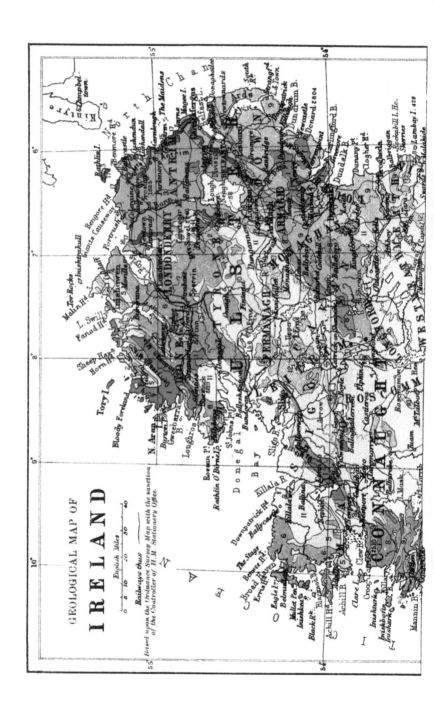

GEOLOGICAL MAP OF
IRELAND

English Miles

0 5 10   20   30   40

Railways thus ⎯⎯⎯

Inset upon the Ordnance Survey Map with the sanction
of the Controller of H.M. Stationery Office.

The Cambridge University Press

Copyright George Philip & Son Ltd.

THE PROVINCES OF IRELAND

Edited by

GEORGE FLETCHER, F.G.S., M.R.I.A.

MUNSTER

MUNSTER

Edited by

GEORGE FLETCHER, F.G.S., M.R.I.A.

With Maps, Diagrams and Illustrations

CAMBRIDGE
AT THE UNIVERSITY PRESS
1921

CAMBRIDGE
UNIVERSITY PRESS

University Printing House, Cambridge CB2 8BS, United Kingdom

Cambridge University Press is part of the University of Cambridge.

It furthers the University's mission by disseminating knowledge in the pursuit of
education, learning and research at the highest international levels of excellence.

www.cambridge.org
Information on this title: www.cambridge.org/9781107511439

© Cambridge University Press 1921

First published 1921
First paperback edition 2015

A catalogue record for this publication is available from the British Library

ISBN 978-1-107-51143-9 Paperback

EDITOR'S NOTE

THE aim of this series is to offer, in a readable form, an account of the physical features of Ireland, and of the economic and social activities of its people. It deals therefore with matters of fact rather than with matters of opinion ; and, for this reason, it has happily been found possible to avoid political controversy. Ireland deserves to be known for her varied scenery, her wealth of archæological and antiquarian lore, her noble educational traditions, and her literary and artistic achievements. The progress and status of Ireland as an agricultural country are recognised and acknowledged, but her industrial potentialities have, until recently, been inadequately studied. The causes of the arrested development of her industries have been frequently dealt with. Her industrial resources, however, demand closer attention than they have hitherto received ; their economic significance has been enhanced by modern applications of scientific discovery and by world-wide economic changes. It is hoped that these pages may contribute to the growing movement in the direction of industrial reconstruction.

It is unusual to enlist the services of many writers in a work of modest dimensions, but it was felt that the more condensed an account, the more necessary was it to secure authoritative treatment. It is hoped that the names of the contributors will afford a sufficient guarantee that the desired end has been achieved. The editorial task of co-ordinating the work of these contributors has been made light and agreeable by their friendly co-operation.

The scope of the volumes and the mode of treatment adopted in them suggest their suitability for use in the higher forms of secondary schools. A notable reform is in course of accomplishment in the teaching of geography. The list of place-names is making room for the more rational study of a country in relation to those who dwell in it, and of these dwellers in relation to their environment.

G. F.

Dublin, *November 1st,* 1921

CONTENTS

ILLUSTRATIONS

MAPS AND DIAGRAMS

Available for download from www.cambridge.org/9781107511439

The illustrations on pp. 14, 16, 23, 28, 33, 41, 43, 44, 45, 47, 49, 50, 137, 141, 145, 146, 148, 157 are reproduced from photographs by Valentine & Sons, Ltd.; those on pp. 21, 159, 160 from photographs by Mr G. Fletcher; that on p. 81 from a photograph by Mr R. Welch; those on pp. 121, 123, 125 from photographs by Mr T. J. Westropp; that on p. 152 from a photograph supplied by Martin Mahony & Bros., Ltd.; those on pp. 162, 169, 170 from photographs by Mr T. F. Geoghegan; that on p. 165 by permission of Viscountess Gough and of Constable & Co., Ltd.

Acknowledgments are due to the Department of Agriculture and Technical Instruction for Ireland, and to the Royal Irish Academy, for permission to use illustrations which have appeared in their publications.

MUNSTER

ANCIENT GEOGRAPHY

THE oldest source of information that we possess regarding the ancient geography of Ireland is contained in the work of the second-century Alexandrian, Ptolemy.

The following are the geographical names which he gives for the region now called the province of Munster: on the West Coast, the River *Dour*, probably one of the inlets of the sea (such as the Kenmare river) at the south-west of Ireland. South of this is the *Hiernos Potamos*—another of these estuaries. This south-west corner of the island was, according to Ptolemy, inhabited by a tribe called the *Vellabroi*, of whom we hear again in the fifth century historian Orosius, but apparently nowhere certainly in Irish traditional history. At the angle was the *Notion Akron*, which perhaps it is hopeless to identify with certainty among the headlands of that complicated coast-line. Turning to the south coast, we meet the *Dabrona* river, with a town *Ivernis* upon it, inhabited by people called *Ivernoi*. The position identifies these with the River Lee (*Sabhrann*[1] in Irish), Cork, and the people there dwelling. The only other place-name is the River *Birgos*, whose name and position identify it with the Barrow (or rather the estuary of the Barrow and Suir). The sea west

[1] On the relation between the names *Dabrona* and *Sabhrann*, see the volume on *Ireland* in this series.

m A

of Ireland Ptolemy calls the *Okeanos Dutikos* ; that to the south, the *Okeanos Vergionos*.

The modern name of Munster, like Ulster and Leinster, is a hybrid, consisting of the Scandinavian suffix -ster (staðr) added to the ancient name Mumha (genitive, Mumhan). From the native name is derived the adjective *Momonian*, found, *e.g.*, in Moore's *Irish Melodies*. The geographical history of this province is extremely complicated, and only the barest outline can be given here. As many as five " Munsters " are recognised by native Irish writers : these are *Tuadh-Mumha* (Anglicised "Thomond," or North Munster); *Ur-Mumha* ("Ormond," East Munster) ; *Mumha Meadhon* (Central Munster) ; *Deas-Mumha* (" Desmond," South Munster) ; and *Iar-Mumha* (West Munster). The first and fourth of these, North and South Munster, were the names of the two provinces of Munster at times when the whole province was sub-divided.

The territorial divisions of Munster were very numerous, and only the most important can be mentioned here. Among them were the *Dál gCais* (pronounced Daul Gash) in Tuadh-Mumha, corresponding to the modern county of Clare. This was the sept to which the king Brian Bóroimhe belonged. They were a Munster people who conquered and occupied this district ; till that event it had been reckoned to Connacht. The *Ui Fidhgheinte*, the descendants of a third century king of Munster, occupied the western part of Co. Limerick. The *Ciar-raighe*, or tribe of Ciar (a son of Fergus and the famous queen Meadhbh of Connacht) ; this was a sept with several branches, one of which settled in Luachair (West Kerry) ; from their name the word " Kerry " is derived. In the barony of Iveragh in

Kerry were settled the *Ui Ráthach*, and round Loch Lein (Killarney) were the *Eoghan-acht*, or people of Eoghan. The *Corcu Duibhne* inhabited the Dingle peninsula (now Corkaguiney) and other parts of the county of Kerry. The ancient territorial name *Bérre* survives in the modern barony of Bear, Co. Cork. Other peoples were the *Muintear Báire* in West Carbury, Co. Cork ; the *Corcu Laighde* (to which the sept of the O'Driscolls belong) in the baronies of Carbury, Beare, and Bantry ; the *Cenéal mBéice*, in the modern barony of Kinalmeaky (the name of which fairly represents the old pronunciation), the *Ui Liatháin*, the descendants of Eochu Liathanach, in the baronies of Barrymore and Kinatalloon, and the *Ui Fothaid*, the descendants of Fothad, in the barony of Iffa and Offa, Co. Tipperary. The *Fir Muighe Féine*, or men of the plain of Fene, are still remembered in the name of the town of Fermoy. An important people was the *Muscraighe*, the descendants of Coirpre Musc, son of Conaire Mór (king of Ireland, according to the Annals, from B.C. 108 to B.C. 39) : these held various territories in Co. Cork, and the baronies of Muskerry preserve their name. We may also mention *Eile*, a territory in the south of King's Co., and north of Tipperary, the *Corcu Athrach* in Tipperary, and the *Déisi* in the baronies of Decies, Co. Waterford.[1]

[1] Most of these names express the descent of the leading family of the territory from an ancestor, either by suffixing a syllable, as -acht, -raighe, which turns the personal name to a tribal designation ; or by prefixing a word such as *Ui*, " descendants," or Dál, Corcu, Cenéal, " race, sept," to the name of the ancestor in the genitive case. The ancestor is either a historical character, or else a mythical being, generally a god : but the subject and the origin of these family names are very obscure.

An important region is Co. Tipperary called Magh
Feimhein (Magh, pronounced something like *mwa*, means
"plain"). It seems to have been a sacred plain, the centre
of the worship of the goddess Brighid. In this plain was
the fairy palace of the mythical king Bodhbh Dearg, of
whom we read in the story of the Children of Lir; and it
was dominated by the mountain called Sliabh na mBan
Finn (now Slievenaman), "hill of the white women"
—unquestionably a group of goddesses; and by
the enormous tumulus *Cnoc Rafann*, the largest artificial earth-mound in Ireland. Though this in outline
resembles a Norman "motte," the exceptional size of
the structure points to the probability of its being much
earlier in origin. It might well have been scarped and
otherwise manipulated by the Normans to serve their
own purposes.

The shiring of Munster is as old as King John's time;
Waterford, Cork, Limerick, Kerry, and Tipperary all
appear as counties in documents of his period. But the
division was not maintained throughout the whole
period of the Plantagenets and Tudors, though the
complex history of the delimitations and names of the
shires and territories would hardly be in place here; it
has little to do with the geography viewed in its bearing
on the population. It is, however, interesting to notice
that Tipperary remained a county palatine (that is,
a county to the administrator of which sovereign power
was delegated) till 1715, when the second Duke of
Ormond was attainted and his jurisdiction abolished.
This was the last relic of a form of government that had
at the beginning of the English occupation been established over most of the country.

POPULATION

According to Beddoe's observations, the population of the province is very mixed in type. Almost the largest proportion of dark-haired and dark-eyed people in Ireland were found in Mallow, Co. Cork; and next to the upper classes in Dublin, among which are probably many of recent English origin, the fairest people in Ireland were found at Charleville, Co. Limerick. The people at other centres lay evenly distributed between these extremes. The colour seems to darken as we proceed from east to west, and from south to north; though there are some exceptions, notably a very dark centre at Cappoquin, Co. Waterford.

In stature the western and southern provinces are on the whole slightly taller than the people of the north and east. The cephalic index (see *Ireland* volume) ranges from 77.1 in West Munster to 76.7 in East Munster; the heads of the Munstermen are distinctly longer than those of the Connachtmen.

The Irish of the province of Munster is perhaps slightly harsher to the ear than that of Connacht, owing to the emphasis laid on the final gutturals: the musical inflexions of the consonantal sounds, though observed in Munster as in the other provinces, are scarcely heard with the delicate perfection of the best Connacht speakers. Owing to the depletion of Munster by emigration, the Irish language has declined in Munster as in Connacht, though it has gained ground in the other two provinces. In 1891 there were 9060 people in Munster who could speak Irish only, and a total number of 307,663 Irish speakers (26.2 per cent. of the total population of the province). In 1901 these figures had sunk respectively to 4387 and 276,268 respectively, and in 1911 to 2766 and 228,694, the latter representing a percentage of 22.1 of the whole population.

TOPOGRAPHY

MUNSTER is the southern province of Ireland, including roughly all the area west and south of Waterford Haven and Galway Bay. It is the largest of the four Irish provinces, having an area of 9536 square miles; Ulster comes next with 8567 square miles, Connaught last with 6802. Munster has also the longest and most diversified coast-line.

The boundary of Munster is a sinuous line running from Galway Bay to Waterford Haven, and separating the counties of Clare, Tipperary, and Waterford on the south from Galway, King's County, Queen's County, Kilkenny, and Wexford on the north. Leaving the southern shore of Galway Bay, the line climbs across the eastern end of the strange grey hills of Burren, descends into the plain of central Clare, climbs again across the desolate moors of the Slieve Aughty range, and descends to the Shannon about half-way along the great lake-like expanse of Lough Derg. Thence it follows that river northward for some seventeen miles, turning eastward again along the line of the Little Brosna river. It zigzags over the limestone pastures as far south as Toomyvara and north again to Roscrea, where it crosses the main watershed of Ireland between the ranges of Slieve Bloom and Devil's Bit, and runs away south-east over rather featureless country between Tipperary and Kilkenny to join the River Suir a couple of miles below the town of Carrick. Thence the river forms the boundary, with Co. Waterford on the southern side and Kilkenny and finally Wexford on the northern,

Munster

(Land over 500 feet elevation shown in black)

till the sea is reached in the spacious estuary of Waterford Haven.

Excepting certain broad flat tracts within the Shannon basin in the west, Munster is a hilly region, and it includes most of the highest mountains found within the country. Three groups rise to over 3000 feet, an elevation elsewhere attained only in Wicklow.

The leading natural features of the province, and also

those relating to human activities—mountain-ranges, valleys, rivers, coast-line, railways, roads, the position of the towns and the distribution of farmed land and of population—are closely bound up with a striking feature which is fully dealt with in the section relating to Geology, but which must be recalled here if the topography of the province is to be understood. In very ancient times this portion of the earth's crust was so crushed together that it became folded—thrown into a series of ridges and furrows, whose direction lay east and west, or north-east and south-west. The covering of limestone which at that time spread over the area has since been to a great extent removed, exposing, especially on the ridges, solid masses of slates and sandstones which lay below. In many of the valleys the limestone still remains. The rivers too, which after the folded area had been smoothed by denudation, flowed southward across it, have had their original sources cut up by the great development of tributaries running from west to east along the bands of slate and limestone remaining in the downfolds. These "subsequent" streams now form, for instance, the more important parts of the Blackwater and the Lee, and the original "consequent" courses are seen only in their final reaches, marked by an abrupt southward bend of the river. On the uplands north of these bends, "beheaded" remnants or dry gaps represent the courses of the former principal streams. For further information on this extremely interesting feature, the classic paper of J. B. Jukes (*Quart. Journ. Geol. Soc.*, vol. xviii., p. 378) ought to be consulted. As a general result of this folding and subsequent denudation we have now a series of great east - and - west ridges and

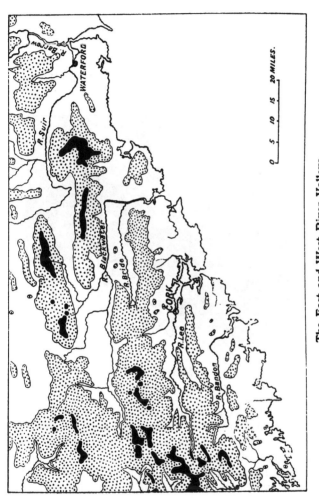

The East-and-West River Valleys

(*Land over 250 feet stippled : land over 1000 feet black*)

valleys, which produce the magnificent mountainous promontories and deep sea-inlets of Cork and Kerry, and determine the direction of the rivers and to a great extent of the railways in the southern part of the province. In the northern portion of

Munster

(*Land over 250 feet elevation shown in black*)

Munster—in Clare, North Tipperary, and Limerick— results of this period of folding are not so obvious. The northern and eastern parts of Tipperary present many areas of typical Central Plain country—wide-stretching limestone pastures with occasional peat-bogs. As we travel south-westward the mountain-ridges and valleys assume more and more a trend in the direc-

tion indicated, till in Western Cork and Kerry the
wilderness of mountain is only interrupted by the deep
sea-filled valleys called Bantry Bay, Kenmare River,
and Dingle Bay. Northern Clare has a type of scenery
of its own, which will be described later ; south of this,
stretching across the Shannon and on to Killarney, is a
wide area of broad, bleak, boggy hills, formed of shales
—the least interesting stretch of country to be found in
Munster.

In Munster the phenomena which characterise the
Irish climate—a slight annual range of temperature, a
high rainfall, and a high degree of humidity—all attain
their most emphatic expression. In January the iso-
therm of 42° F. includes more than half the province,
while in South Cork and South Kerry the temperature
during that (the coldest) winter month is above 44°.
The summers are correspondingly cool, the average
July temperature of Munster being between 59° and 60°.
As regards precipitation, while in Tipperary this is
moderate—about 40 inches—it rises as one passes
south-west, so that the 50-inch curve includes West Cork
and the greater part of Kerry. As one approaches the
main mountain mass of Kerry, 60 inches and 70 inches
are passed, and among the Reeks the rainfall is probably
much higher even than this. The effect of the perennial
humidity is evidenced in a remarkable manner by the
vegetation ; nowhere in the British Isles do moisture-
loving mosses and ferns flourish so luxuriantly as in
Kerry. The prevailing westerly winds, which are the
cause of this excessive moisture, are also responsible
for the absence of trees in the more exposed western
tracts, and of even bushes on many of the islands and

headlands ; though where shelter is afforded luxuriant vegetation at once puts in an appearance.

MOUNTAINS

Far to the eastward, in Co. Waterford, the Comeraghs form a highly picturesque group of hills of irregular shape. They present an imposing series of lofty sandstone scarps, and their summits lie mostly between 2000 and 2600 ft. The Comeraghs derive their name from the deep coombs, embosoming lakes, which form their most striking feature. The most notable of these, Coomshingaun, presents a sheer cliff over 1000 ft. in height, dropping into a deep lakelet at its foot.

North of the Comeraghs, across the valley of the Suir, in Tipperary, the broad cone of Slievenaman (2295 ft.) rises solitary and dominates the country for many miles.

Not many miles west of the Comeraghs, the Knockmealdown Mountains form a bold east-and-west ridge, dropping into the Suir valley on the north and the valley of the Blackwater on the south. They present a bold row of peaks of over 2000 ft., the highest point being 2609 ft. A picturesque road climbs across the centre of the range, ascending to over 1100 ft.

A few miles north-west of the Knockmealdowns, across a limestone trough in which lie the celebrated Mitchelstown Caves, a loftier east-and-west ridge, the Galtees, towers up, with steep slopes especially to the north and west. They attain in Galtymore an elevation of 3015 ft.—a height reached elsewhere in Ireland only in Kerry and Wicklow. This is a compact and picturesque mountain group, with several fine coombs embosoming lakes on the northern slopes. Lower hills (up to 1700 ft.), known as the Ballyhoura Mountains, continue far to the west, and are conspicuous from the train about Charleville, where the line to Cork passes round their flank and turns south to Mallow.

In North Tipperary, some 20 to 30 miles north of the Galtees, there is a large area of hilly country stretching north-westward to the Shannon at Killaloe and north-eastward to the Devil's Bit, near the borders of King's County. Much the highest point is Slieve Kimalta, or Keeper Hill (2278 ft.). A western outlier of this range, the Arra Mountains, separated from the main mass by a deep narrow valley—possibly an old course of the Shannon—forms the eastern side of the deep Shannon gorge, where that river, passing between high hills, at length escapes from the plain and plunges down from Lough Derg to the sea.

The western side of the Shannon gorge is formed by a group of hills known as Slieve Bernagh (1746 ft.). Though separated from the Arra Mountains by the Shannon and Lough Derg, these two really form a single hill - group, through which the river has cut its way.

North of Slieve Bernagh again, in Clare, there is a large area of bleak hilly country rising here and there to well over 1000 ft., known as Slieve Aughty.

All the hill-groups which have been mentioned so far are more or less isolated uplands surrounded by limestone lowlands, and formed of older slates and sandstones (Silurian or Devonian) which have been pushed up and now impend, dark and heathery, over the limestone grass-lands.

South of the valley of the Blackwater the limestone remains only in a few narrow valley bottoms, and we find ourselves in almost continuously broken country, which gets more and more mountainous as we go westward. The first portion of the hilly country which we meet is the upland which lies between the Blackwater and Lee valleys in Co. Cork. Through a transverse "through" valley near its eastern end the main line of railway finds its way southward to Cork (see p. 26).

Cottages in the Killarney Mountains

Further west the hills attain the dignity of mountains (Boggeragh and Derrynasaggart Mountains), where Caherbarnagh (2239 ft.) and The Paps (2284 ft.) look down on the railway between Millstreet and Killarney. Beyond that the broad ridge is interrupted by the interesting flat-bottomed narrow valley, overhung by high hills, through which the railway and road find their way to Kenmare. The question of the origin of this pass is dealt with in the section on Geology. Westward the hills divide into two main groups, one on either side of Kenmare river, and present, not a simple chain, but a wild tangle of mountains. The southern mass runs south-westward for over 50 miles between the Kenmare river and Bantry Bay, till it terminates in the lofty cliffs of Dursey Island. For 30 miles — from the Macroom-Killarney road to Hungry Hill—the watershed (which is also the Cork-Kerry boundary) keeps above the 1000-ft. contour, and the three roads which cross the range climb over high passes by the aid of numerous zigzags to ease their gradient. Many summits rise to 2000-2200 ft., the loftiest being Knockboy (2321 ft.). The middle portion of the range is known as the Caha Mountains and the lower western extremity as Slieve Miskish. Towns or villages among the hills there are none ; the centres of population, which are small and few, lie along the coast at the foot of the mountains—on the northern side Kenmare, and on the southern Glengarriff and Castletown Berehaven.

The northern of the two mountain masses forms similarly a great promontory, as long (some 40 miles) as the other, and twice as broad. It has the sea-inlet called the Kenmare river for its south-eastern boundary and the broader Dingle Bay on its north-western side. On the north a deep narrow trough of limestone runs from Killarney westward to Dingle Bay, down which the River Flesk, which drains the Lakes of Killarney, meanders to the sea. This tract of some 600 square miles is filled with mountains, which include the highest peaks in Ireland. Far to the east, between Killarney and the Kenmare valley, the broad mass of

Mangerton (2756 ft.) dominates a number of lower summits.

Westward a few miles, across the deep gash in which lies the Upper Lake of Killarney, Macgillicuddy's Reeks rise head and shoulders above the surrounding

Macgillicuddy's Reeks, Killarney

sea of hills. These are a beautiful group of lofty cones, with steep sides and many imposing cliff ranges, and deep coombs in which lie dark tarns. The loftiest, Carrantuohill, the highest mountain in Ireland, attains 3414 ft., and several of the other peaks exceed 3000 ft. At the east end of the Reeks the famous Gap of Dunloe, through which a road runs, separates them from the

Purple Mountain group which looks down on the Lower Lake.

Running south-west from the Reeks, an irregular chain of peaks of over 2000 ft. forms a barrier almost to the extremity of the promontory at Derrynane. Lower ground along the north-western base of this ridge allows a road to traverse the whole length of the promontory in a parallel direction. North of this line again high hills rise and stretch on to the coast of Dingle Bay.

The low limestone depression that runs from Killarney to the sea at Dingle Bay zigzags back eastward to Castleisland and back again to the sea at Tralee.

Westward from this valley, and quite cut off from the continuous mass of mountains which have just been dealt with, a wild mountain chain protrudes far into the Atlantic, terminating in the Blasket Islands, which are themselves steep mountain peaks rising out of the ocean. For 45 miles this highland extends, with a breadth of 6 to 12 miles. The hills divide themselves into three groups : in the east Slieve Mish (2796 ft.), in the centre the Beenoskee group (2713 ft.), and beyond that the glorious knife-edge ridge of Brandon (3127 ft.).

Inland, to the east of the Dingle promontory, a large area of rather low, boggy hills extends over parts of Kerry, Cork, and Limerick, stretching northward to the Shannon. Many flattish summits rise to from 1000 to 1400 ft. The district is rather desolate, and the soft, shaly rocks produce no features of interest. The same type of surface is continued northward across the Shannon into Central Clare. Continuing northward we enter, in the barony of

m B

Burren, a very different and extremely interesting upland.

The Burren is formed of limestone hills of about 1000 ft. in height (Slieve Elva rises to 1134 ft.). As viewed from a distance, their outlines are gently rounded, but among the hills some deep passes and lofty cliff ranges are to be found. The feature which gives this upland its peculiar character is the limestone that almost everywhere is quite bare of covering. For mile after mile the grey rock, its surface seamed and carved by rain into fantastic shapes, lies open to the sky. The beds lie horizontally, and terrace rises above terrace.

The rain sinks into innumerable deep fissures which seam the rock, and streams or standing water are almost absent from the area : the drainage is underground, and in places the water may be seen gushing from the rocks at sea-level. So damp is the climate that the absence of soil and stream does not prevent a luxuriant vegetation from flourishing wherever a little vegetable mould has been left ; and the bare country is actually in much demand for sheep-grazing, so sweet and abundant are the grasses which spring from every chink. The vegetation includes a large number of very interesting plants, as described on p. 84.

RIVERS AND LAKES

The river systems of Munster divide themselves into two groups. In the northern half the Shannon is the dominating feature, flowing south-westward through a wide plain only occasionally interrupted by hills, and draining the whole of Limerick, the greater part of Clare, and half of North Tipperary. In the southern half the drainage has been profoundly affected by the east-and-west folding of the country, to which reference was made on p. 8, and the rivers conform in a very definite manner to conditions imposed by this ancient crumpling of the crust.

Munster touches the Shannon first where the Little Brosna river, separating King's County from Tipperary, runs into the main stream at Meelick, where one of the few rapids of the Shannon interrupts the placid course of the river, and locks have been built to assist navigation. Thence the broad slow stream meanders down to Portumna, where it enters Lough Derg, the lower two-thirds of which belong wholly to Munster. Lough Derg is some 22 miles in length, and generally about $1\frac{1}{2}$ mile wide, with occasional inlets on either hand which increase the width to about twice that amount—at one point to 9 miles.

Lough Derg is, in fact, a great river expansion rather than a lake, and has been produced mainly by solution of the limestone which forms the greater part of its shores. The upper end is shallow, with flat limestone country on either hand, but as one proceeds down its winding island-studded course the scenery gets bolder on account of the approach of uplands which close in on either hand, till at the lower end the lake lies in a gorge between steep hills. These hills are formed of slates, and the fact that the river has cut this deep gorge through them instead of following a different course eastward or westward across the low limestone country is the most remarkable feature of Shannon topography. Its course is believed to date from a time when the great limestone area to the north stood much higher, so that the route over Lough Derg formed the easiest

way to the sea. The plain was lowered by denudation as the Shannon cut its way downward, the rate
being determined by the rate at which the gorge
could be cut, since this was the outlet for the removed
material. As seen now the topography of the middle
Shannon is very striking. The traveller standing at
Athlone sees all round him nothing but plain, save to
the southward, where a distant rim of hills breaks the
line of the horizon. Towards these hills the river
takes its course. As one advances, the hills close in
to right and left, and still the river goes straight on
for their centre. One gets the idea that the Shannon
is running uphill. As Lough Derg is entered, it is clear
that the stream is heading for a deep narrow notch
which appears far in front. Presently the hills approach
so as to descend to the water's edge on either hand.
Their dark heathery summits rise to 1500 and 1700 ft.
on the east and west. And then at Killaloe the lake-
like expanse narrows and the Shannon goes foaming
over ledges of rock to resume further down its placid
flow over the level limestones. Having in its middle
course pursued its way for 130 miles over the Limestone
Plain with a fall of only 51 ft., it now drops 97 ft. in
18 miles to reach sea-level at Limerick. The great
estuary which it then forms, over 50 miles in length,
is described on p. 31.

The Suir, rising in the hilly region of North
Tipperary, flows southward through flat limestone
country past Thurles, and at Caher passes close by the
eastern end of the high ridge of the Galtees. Ten miles
further on, at Newcastle, it finds itself in a cul-de-sac,
caused by the dominance of the east-and-west ridges
already referred to frequently. The Suir may at one

time, when the limestone floor occupied a higher level, have flowed on between the Knockmealdowns and Comeraghs to the sea at Dungarvan or Youghal. But now, carried off eastward by a tributary of the old consequent river that has its lower reach in Waterford Haven, it follows the limestone trough, above which the more resisting sandstones form mountain land,

Weir and Sluices, Killaloe

bends sharply northward, and then turns eastward along the base of the Comeraghs, through Clonmel and Carrick-on-Suir (where it becomes tidal) to meet the sea at Waterford Haven. The monotony of its marshy upper reaches is fully compensated by the beauty of its middle course about Caher and Clonmel, with the lofty ridges of the Galtees, Knockmealdowns, and Comeraghs rising around.

The west-to-east course of the Blackwater is one of the most striking features of the geography of the South of Ireland. Rising on the boggy Coal-measure hills of North Kerry, it flows south for some 10 miles to the foot of the high hills which are grouped round Caherbarnagh (2239 ft.). Then it strikes the upper end of a limestone trough which it follows almost due eastward for nearly 60 miles to Cappoquin. Then, deserting this trough, which continues eastward to meet the sea at Dungarvan, it turns abruptly southward, cuts through the barrier of slates which all the way has formed its southern bank, and flows for 15 miles through an interesting and picturesque gorge in places 400 to 500 ft. deep to reach the sea at Youghal. This east-and-west trough is the best marked of those which characterise the South of Ireland, and is utilised from end to end by railways and main roads. A minor parallel valley lying a few miles south of the eastern part of the trough is occupied by an important tributary, the River Bride, which enters the main stream a few miles below Cappoquin. The gorge between Cappoquin and Youghal represents one of the few portions of the ancient north-to-south drainage channels which has been continuously occupied by a river. In old days it bore to the sea the rains which fell on areas to the northward ; possibly the Suir once continued its southern course, and passing between the Knockmealdowns and Comeraghs, debouched through this gorge ; now the lowering of the limestone troughs by solution has diverted it to the eastward, and the old gorge serves to discharge waters which, in their turn, reach the ocean far to the east of their gathering-grounds.

The Lee and the Bandon Rivers reproduce on a smaller scale, but still in a striking way, the features just described in the case of the Blackwater, save that their

The Lee at St Patrick's Bridge, Cork

courses no longer lie to so great an extent on limestone. The Lee flows from the romantic mountain-lake of Gouganebarra, only 9 miles north of the head of Bantry Bay, and runs eastward past Macroom to Cork, where it reaches sea-level; there, like the Blackwater, it turns south and cuts through ridges of slate to the ocean; its complicated tidal portion, which forms Cork Harbour, is dealt with on p. 46. The Bandon river has a somewhat similar but more irregular course; it likewise flows eventually southward into the Atlantic between bold headlands, forming Kinsale Harbour.

While the most famous lake in Munster is at Killarney, the largest is Lough Derg, which lies within the province, save that the northern part of its western shore belongs to Galway. The features of this large expanse of water have already been sketched in the description of the River Shannon (p. 19). A few additional particulars may be added here. In the limestone portion of the lake—that is, the whole save the southern end—the shores and bottom are very irregular, as is usual in lakes due to solution, and the depth not great. Islands and reefs abound, and the shores are low and rocky. The greatest width—nine miles, measured east and west from Scarriff Bay and Youghal Bay—corresponds with the southern edge of the limestone. The east-and-west shore-line south of this expansion marks the incoming of the non-soluble slates, and the lake immediately contracts into a deep narrow gut, about 1 mile across and 100 ft. in depth, with high banks. The excessive deepening here is probably due to glacial action.

The lakes of Killarney are described on p. 39.

TRAFFIC ROUTES

Railways arc morc scnsitivc than roads to thc configuration of the surface of the country, because the heavy loads drawn by locomotives tell severely when hills are encountered. Thus, while a gradient of 1 in 30 is considered reasonable on a main road, 1 in 100 is looked on as a severe hill on a line of railway. Thus it comes that, as a study of a map of any hilly district will show, the railways follow so far as possible river valleys wherever the surface is undulating, often reaching by a circuitous but level route a point arrived at by road by a bold climb through hills. These considerations apply in Ireland to the province of Munster in particular, because in this area, especially in the southern two-thirds of it, a series of strong ridges and valleys characterise the surface, running east and west, or north-east and south-west. These are the visible effects of ancient crushing and folding of this portion of the earth's crust, as explained on a previous page. Thus easy east-and-west routes are available for the railways, but practicable north-and-south routes are few. The sketch-map on p. 27 will show how the railways have conformed to the existing physical conditions.

Taking Cork, the capital of the province, we see (p. 9) that easy routes to east and west lie in the Lee valley and its continuation to Youghal, and in the valley of the Bandon river. These are availed of in the lines to Macroom and Coachford on the west, and in the line to Youghal on the east ; while the Cork, Bandon, and South Coast Railway, by crossing a low ridge on the south, utilises the parallel Bandon valley for a considerable distance. On the other hand, a high broad ridge stretching east and west between the valleys of the Lee and Blackwater bars the way to the north. The outflanking of its barrier is not practicable, and it has to be overcome by a heroic climb to the north-west, where a transverse depression (one of the ancient north-and-south river valleys referred to on p. 8), and a north and south consequent valley on either side, allow the ridge to be crossed at an elevation of about 500 ft. From the station at Cork, with its long curved platforms, the line, commencing to ascend at once, plunges through a three quarter mile tunnel under the hill on which the barracks stand, and skirting the northern side of the city, climbs steeply away, the gradient being for a time 1 in 60, an exceptional slope for a main line; in spite of the power of modern locomotives, a second engine has often to be used here. Once the summit is reached, 13 miles from Cork, an easy descent leads to the Blackwater valley and Mallow, whence the way is open to Dublin. As will be seen from the map (p. 27). no other railway has been constructed across these east-and-west folds; but far on either hand, at Waterford and Killarney, other lines get northward by passing round their ends.

The railways of northern Munster—mostly branches of the Great Southern and Western system—need no special mention. The nature of the surface allows of a loose network of lines, of which Limerick is the centre; from that city railways radiate in five directions. Waterford, in the extreme east of the province, is another important railway centre and port, with six lines of railway radiating

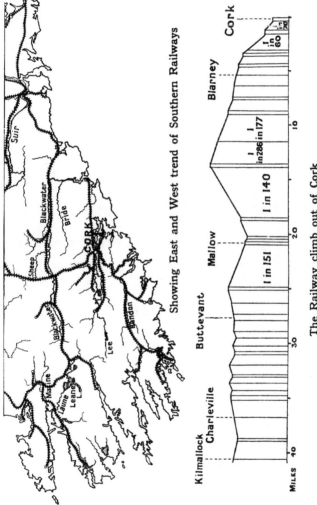

Showing East and West trend of Southern Railways

The Railway climb out of Cork

from it.   Extensive recent improvements here, connected with the establishment of a fast passenger
service *via* Rosslare (30 miles to the eastward) and
Fishguard in Wales have resulted in all the lines,
except the short one to Tramore, being brought into one
station.   A corresponding improvement at Cork has
recently linked up the Bandon line on the west with
the lines to Dublin and Queenstown (now Cobh).

Listowel and Ballybunion Railway

Special mention may be made of the Listowel and
Ballybunion Railway in North Kerry, since it is the only
line in the British Isles constructed on the mono-rail
system.   The permanent way consists of a single
elevated rail supported on trestles ; the equilibrium of
the rolling stock is maintained by its being built to hang
down on each side, like panniers on a horse's back.
The line is about 10 miles in length, and pays a good
dividend to the shareholders.

Railway construction has now been pushed far into

the western wilds, and many of the more remote places, such as Lehinch, Kilkee, Dingle, Valencia, Kenmare, and Skull are connected with the main systems. Some of these lines are broad gauge (*i.e.* 5 ft. 3 in.) and others narrow gauge (3 ft.), and most of them pass through wild and beautiful scenery.

There are practically no canals in Munster. The large and deep estuaries of some of the rivers—which represent the seaward continuation of the present river valleys, now drowned by a sinking of the land— provide natural waterways, some of which are much used ; for instance, the noble estuary of the Shannon, extending for over 50 miles from Loop Head to Limerick, and the harbours of Cork and Waterford. The tidal part of the Suir is used, giving a sea connection with Carrick-on-Suir ; but the only artificial waterway in the province of any importance is that by which the Shannon has been made navigable in its steep descent from Lough Derg to the sea, where, after an almost level course, it falls 97 ft. in 18 miles.

ROUND THE COAST

Starting at the boundary of Clare and Galway, on Galway Bay, a low coast with deep indentations, after the manner of the limestone, leads to Ballyvaughan, a village situated in a sheltered bay, from which a steamer connection with Galway is maintained—a necessary accommodation, as the nearest railway station (Ardrahan) is 16 miles distant. Around Bally- vaughan and westward to the Atlantic, and filling the greater part of the barony of Burren, there rise the hills whose strange appearance catches the eye of the traveller at Galway or on the moors of southern Connemara. They are formed of bare limestone, rising terrace above terrace over many miles to a height of 1000 ft. or more. A good road follows the coast westward along the shore, which towards Black Head becomes steep. Rounding the headland, which marks the entrance of Galway Bay, we see the Aran Islands, which are low shelves of the same limestone rock, and which give us a measure of the former extent of this formation. Though geologically a part of Clare, these islands belong politically to Galway, and are dealt with in the Connaught volume of the present series.

Beyond Fisherstreet the limestone gives way to beds of shale and flagstones, and the coast rises into the finest range of cliffs to be found in Ireland.

The grand rock-wall, known as the Cliffs of Moher, extends for several miles along the coast, attaining an elevation of over 650 ft. On account of the tabular nature of the rock the top is flat, and one can safely approach the edge and look down the great perpendicular wall to where the Atlantic swell surges round its base. Several tall outlying pinnacles rising from the water enhance the effect.

Beyond the Cliffs of Moher there is a sharp indentation of the coast, forming Liscannor Bay, in which stands the little watering-place of Lahinch. Thence a storm-swept rocky coast, with occasional sandy bays, trends south-westward for nearly 40 miles to Loop Head. Towards the south, where stands Kilkee, much frequented by summer visitors, dark cliffs of shale, fantastically carved by the sea, prevail.

Between Loop Head and Kerry Head, which projects 10 miles to the southward, the great estuary of the

Shannon opens. From its mouth to Limerick, where the river ceases to be tidal, the distance is 54 miles. During the greater part of this distance the Shannon maintains a breadth of from 1 to 3 miles. In the lower part of the estuary the gravelly shores are diversified and picturesque, with many villages along the water's edge; while further up the land on either side is lower, its banks become muddy, and great areas of marshy pasture fringe the river. Two-thirds way up on the northern shore the wide muddy estuary of the Fergus opens out, studded with islands. The Fergus itself is quite a small stream, but its estuary, which is a flooded limestone lowland, would do credit to a large river. As a result of the marshy nature of the lands bordering the Shannon in the upper part of the estuary, the towns and villages are no longer situated on its banks, but lie some miles back from the river till we come to Limerick, where the ground on either side is firm.

For communication between Limerick and the many villages along the estuary, this fine waterway is availed of, and steamers run along its whole length. Half-way down its southern bank, Foynes is connected by rail with Limerick. Far down the northern shore a narrow-gauge line (the West Clare Railway) runs from Kilrush northward, and connects by a circuitous route with Ennis.

Crossing the Shannon southward we enter the county of Kerry. Ballybunnion, which faces across to Loop Head, is the terminus of the mono-rail line that runs inland to Listowel. Kerry Head is a high promontory greatly exposed to the ocean. Thence a low indented coast leads past the deep-water pier at Fenit to Tralee, an important town at the head of the shallow Tralee Bay.

Westward from Tralee stretches the most northern of the great mountain promontories which lend such grandeur to the scenery of Kerry and West Cork. The origin and meaning of these has been touched on already in the general description of the province, and is more fully explained in the section devoted to Geology. The Dingle promontory is joined to the main mass of the land by a low depression filled with limestone; a rise of 100 ft. in the level of the sea would convert it into an island. The northern shore of the promontory is exceedingly varied, the leading features being the long Castlegregory peninsula, where low limestone reefs run far into the sea; and the huge precipices where Brandon drops into the ocean. The Blasket Islands, off the end of the promontory, are high and rugged, and are tenanted by a very primitive community. The south shore includes two safe land-locked harbours at Ventry and Dingle: on the shores of the latter stands the town of Dingle, an important fishing centre.

The upper end of Dingle Bay, which separates this from the next mountain promontory, is shallow, almost closed by sand-dunes, and much encumbered by sand-banks: it is known as Castlemaine Harbour.

Next, repeating many of the features of the Dingle promontory, a wilderness of mountains and lakes, 18 miles across and twice that in length, intervenes between Dingle Bay and Kenmare river. A line of railway runs down its northern shore through Caherciveen to Valencia Harbour. Valencia Island, which lies close inshore, is well known as the terminus of several of the transatlantic telegraph cables. From Valencia a beautifully wild coast continues to the entrance of the Kenmare river, which is not a river at all, but a long, deep, tapering sea-inlet running in through the mountains for about 27 miles. The town of Sneem, and Parknasilla with its large hotel, stand on its northern shore. At the head is Kenmare, a busy

Valencia Harbour, Co. Kerry

market town, and the terminus of a branch railway from the main line to Killarney.

A third great mountain promontory now intervenes between Kenmare river and Bantry Bay, filled with high hills, and presenting a magnificent coast-line. It terminates in Dursey Island. Half-way down its northern shore we pass from Kerry into Cork. On its southern shore, in Bantry Bay, sheltered behind Bere Island, is Bere Haven, an important naval base.

m C

At the head of Bantry Bay is Glengarriff, one of the loveliest spots in Ireland, with wooded islands studding the calm, deep water. The south shore of Bantry Bay runs far out as a narrow mountainous promontory, with the deep, narrow inlet of Dunmanus Bay on its

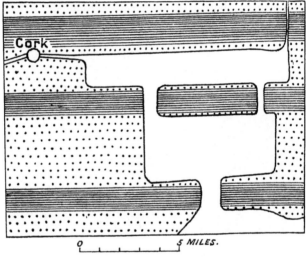

Cork Harbour—diagrammatic
Dotted areas = limestone troughs ; shaded areas = sandstone ridges

other side. Beyond that the land runs out again to Mizen Head, the most southern point of the Irish mainland. Thence an exceedingly broken coast runs eastward past Cape Clear (on Clear Island) away to Cork Harbour. Bold headlands alternate with sheltered inlets with little fishing towns nestling on their banks. The most conspicuous of the projections of the coast

are Toe Head, Galley Head, Seven Heads, and the Old
Head of Kinsale. The most important port is Kinsale,
which has a large fishing industry. It lies near the
mouth of the Bandon river, and was formerly a fortified harbour of importance : but the increased size of

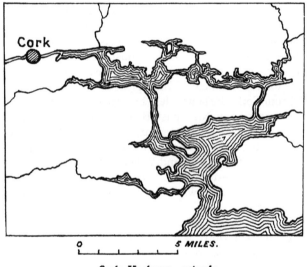

Cork Harbour—actual

modern ships has led to a transfer of much of its trade
to Cork and Queenstown (Cobh).

Cork Harbour, which is now reached, has already been
described as to its mode of origin on p. 8, and is further
referred to on p. 46. The main harbour, inside the
mile-wide entrance, is a considerable expanse of water,
with a deep channel through it. Queenstown (Cobh)
is boldly situated facing the entrance. Two channels cut

through the ridge in which it stands, the left-hand one running up towards Midleton, the deeper right-hand one continuing past Passage to a second expansion known as Lough Mahon, which has muddy arms spreading far to east and west. Thence ships pass in a north-westerly direction up the narrow River Lee to Cork. Cork Harbour and Queenstown (Cobh) derive much of their importance from being a port of call for American mail steamers. But the huge increase in size of modern liners is beginning to tell against even this spacious port, which is now considered by some captains as not safe for the handling of their gigantic ships.

From Cork Harbour a less broken and less precipitous coast runs on E.N.E. past Ballycotton Bay to the old town of Youghal, situated at the mouth of the River Blackwater. Just inside its mouth the estuary expands, forming a safe harbour, and Youghal stands picturesquely on the steep western bank. The Blackwater is tidal and forms a useful waterway as far as Cappoquin, 15 miles to the northward.

In crossing the Blackwater we pass from Co. Cork into Co. Waterford, which possesses a varied coast-line. A bold shore runs from Youghal to Dungarvan Harbour, a rather large shallow bay with its upper part almost cut off by a straight spit of sand which extends from the southern shore nearly to the town of Dungarvan on the opposite side. Eastward, a stretch of coast, boldly precipitous in places, brings us to Tramore Bay, broad and sandy, with the watering-place of Tramore at its western end. As at Dungarvan, the inner part of the bay is almost cut off by a long sand-spit, in this case much broader and more mature.

A few miles further on we reach the broad entrance

of Waterford Haven. The River Barrow, coming
from the north, already joined by the Nore, meets the
River Suir, coming from the west, at a point 10 miles
from the sea, and the combined streams flow southward
through a wide, deep estuary into the Atlantic. The
important port and railway centre of Waterford stands
on the south bank of the Suir, about 6 miles above
its junction with the Barrow. The Suir is tidal as far
as Carrick-on-Suir, and is used as a waterway ; and the
Barrow is tidal as far as St Mullins, in Co. Carlow, whence
the river is canalised for a great part of its length, and
eventually joins the main line of the Grand Canal some
20 miles from Dublin.

Waterford Haven divides Munster from Leinster,
so our coastal survey terminates here.

The interesting Aran Islands, lying in Galway Bay
between Clare and Connemara, belong politically to
Galway, and are referred to in the Connaught volume
of this series. South of them, no island of importance
is met with till we reach the Blaskets, which form
the seaward prolongation of the mountainous Dingle
promontory, and are themselves almost mountains in
height. The Great Blasket, much the largest of the
group and the only one which is inhabited, is a
narrow ridge like a knife-edge, 4 miles long and nearly
1000 ft. high. At its eastern extremity, where a little
shelter is available, a colony of houses clings to the
steep slope, surrounded by a patch of cultivation.
On the most westerly of the group, the Tearaght, a light-
house stands. Some 20 miles to the southward, off
Bolus Head, two lovely pinnacled rocks, the Skelligs,
rise many hundreds of feet into the air. Another outlying rock familiar to those who go down to the sea in

ships is the Fastnet, lying off Cape Clear. Inshore are many larger islands, mostly wild and cliff-bound, though less romantic than the distant lighthouse-guarded rocks just mentioned. Valencia Island, Bere Island, and Clear Island are the most important. On the East Cork and Waterford coasts islands are very few and small.

COUNTIES AND TOWNS

Six counties are included within the province ; several of these are of exceptional size, so that Munster has an area of 9536 square miles—an area larger than that of Leinster with its twelve counties, or Ulster with its nine.

	Area in Square Miles.	Population.
Kerry . . .	1,853	159,691
Cork	2,890	392,104
Waterford . . .	721	83,966
Tipperary . . .	1,660	152,433
Limerick . . .	1,064	143,069
Clare	1,348	104,232
Total . .	9,536	1,035,495

Of these, Tipperary alone lies entirely inland. Limerick along the greater part of its northern edge borders the broad Shannon estuary ; the remaining four counties present an extended and much indented front to the ocean.

Co. Kerry

The wildest and most diversified county in Ireland, on account of its long, fiord-like sea-inlets, its high mountain ranges, and its beautiful lakes and woods.

The area from Killarney north to the Shannon is alone rather dull, as the high ribs of sandstone and slate which produce the bold features of the rest of the county are here replaced by softer shales, which weather into low, bog-smothered hills. The rivers of Kerry are short and rapid, and among the mountains small lakes and tarns are numerous.

Tralee (10,300), the county town, is situated at the shallow head of a bay far to the westward. The small stream on which it stands has been widened and deepened to allow of the passage of coasting craft to the town, but larger vessels berth at Fenit, a few miles westward. Killorglin (7443) is an important marketing centre. Dingle (1884), the most westerly town in Europe, lies in a sheltered bay near the extremity of the mountainous Dingle Peninsula. Killarney (5976) is inland, near the beautiful lakes of the same name, with wild mountains to the west and south and low, boggy uplands to the north. Kenmare (1034) is beautifully situated at the head of the noble sea-inlet known as Kenmare river : steamers berth a short distance below the town. Castleisland (1333) and Listowel (3409) lie in the less picturesque country to the north.

The famous Lakes of Killarney lie at the eastern end of Macgillicuddy's Reeks, the loftiest mountain range in Ireland. They consist of a tolerably large sheet of water, the Lower Lake or Lough Leane, the small and scarcely distinct Muckross Lake, and another small and very irregular sheet of water, the Upper Lake; the last lies among high hills, and is connected with the others by a broad slow stream, the Long Reach. Different agencies have been at work in the production of these lakes. The Lower Lake and

Muckross Lake lie on the limestone where it abuts on
the older non-soluble slates which form the Reeks—

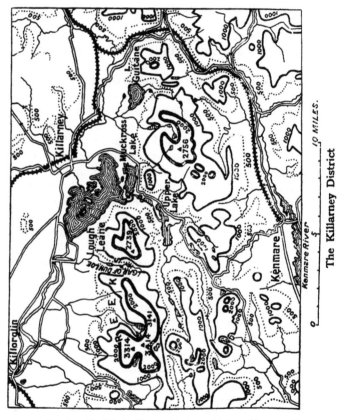

The Killarney District

just as the Corrib-Mask-Conn chain of lakes lies on the
edge of the Central Plain where it rests against the old
rocks of Connemara and West Mayo. The eastern

Torc Waterfall, Killarney

shores of the Lower Lake, where the limestone prevails, are low and deeply indented, while the western shore, formed of slates, is steep and straight. The Lower Lake owes its origin chiefly to solution, the limestone having been dissolved in the irregular manner character-istic of such action. The Upper Lake is quite different in character, with shores formed of smoother and rounder ribs of rock which plunge into deep water. Its basin is the result of the scooping action of land ice during the Glacial Period. The presence of the towering summits of the Reeks immediately to the west produces much shelter from wind, and also a heavy rainfall; the position of Killarney relative to the Atlantic, which surrounds Kerry on three sides, tends to remarkable mildness of climate. Hence we find in this area beautiful woods which harbour plants and animals belonging to regions far southward—to Spain and the Mediterranean; and hence also we find there a wonderful luxuriance of ferns and mosses, and other plants which love continual moisture.

Co. Cork

The largest county in Ireland, and of very diversified surface. In the east and north are expanses of typical Central Plain country—gently undulating limestone pastures. These are interrupted by east-and-west ridges of sandstones and slates, with picturesque river valleys between. As we pass westward these ridges increase in height and width, till in Western Cork they occupy the whole surface, producing wild and beautiful mountain scenery which continues and develops further in Kerry. The coast-line, as in Kerry, is exceedingly broken, with long and deep sea-inlets in the west.

Cork, West End

Cork (76,673), the capital of the province, lies among cultivated hills where the east-and-west valley of the Lee dips below sea-level. It is a busy port and railway centre. The railway from Dublin, dropping steeply into the valley (see p. 26), reaches the station through a

Grand Parade, Cork

long tunnel, and runs on to Queenstown (Cobh) and Youghal. Further west, the Cork, Bandon, and South Coast Railway has its terminus : it serves a large area, penetrating to the Kerry border. A loop line now connects these two systems. A shorter line runs to Macroom. The port accommodates steamers of considerable tonnage, but the largest boats lie in the open water of Cork Harbour, some miles down. The city had its origin as a fortified post of the Danes on a small island in the

Queenstown (Cobh) Cathedral and Church Hill, Co. Cork

Lee, following on the ecclesiastical settlement founded there by St Fin Barre in the seventh century. It has spread far beyond these narrow confines, and in some parts has climbed up the steep hills that rise over the river, so that the houses rise tier above tier. The appearance of the principal street is bright and busy, and many of the public buildings are good.

Cork Harbour is an extremely irregular arm of the sea with a narrow entrance, 12 miles in length from Cork city to the open sea. It represents the sunken continuation of the Lee valley, and really consists of two drowned limestone troughs lying between three east-and-west ridges of slate, through which north-and-south passages have been cut by rivers. The first of these ridges rises along the northern edge of the area, by Cork and Midleton ; the second across the centre, forming Great Island, on which stands the important port of Queenstown (Cobh) (8209) ; and the third across the mouth, where the twin forts are perched high above the sea. Its structure is illustrated on pp. 34, 35. Youghal (5648) is a fishing port and summer resort at the mouth of the Blackwater, in the extreme east. Kinsale (4020), Clonakilty (2961), Skibbereen (3021), and Bantry (3159) lie on the western coast. Inland, Dunmanway (1619) and Bandon (3122) are on the Bandon river, and Macroom (2717) on the Lee. Along the picturesque valley of the Blackwater are Kanturk (1518), Mallow (4452) (an important railway junction) and Fermoy (6863). Northward, in the more level limestone country, are Buttevant (1754) and Charleville (1925). Mitchelstown (2268) is in the north-east, at the southern base of the Galtee mountains.

Queenstown (Cobh) Harbour

Co. Waterford

A fertile and picturesque area. The River Suir forms much of the northern boundary, and the Blackwater traverses the eastern part of the county. Much of the centre and east is occupied by the lofty ridges of the Comeragh (2597 ft.) and Knockmealdown (2609 ft.) mountains. The coast-line is extensive, and often cliff-bound. On the eastern edge, the spacious inlet of Waterford Haven forms the estuary of the Suir, Barrow, and Nore. The western limit of the coast is the smaller inlet of Youghal Harbour, through which the Blackwater reaches the ocean.

Waterford (27,464) is one of the foremost cities and ports in the southern half of Ireland. It stands on the southern bank of the Suir, 6 miles above the point where that stream joins the Barrow and 17 miles from the open sea. It has a considerable export trade, and is a railway centre of increasing importance. Part of the town, including the railway station, lies on the north or Kilkenny side of the river, across which a new ferro-concrete bridge has recently replaced the old wooden toll bridge. Portlaw (947) stands near the Suir ; Dungarvan (4977) is at the head of the shallow Dungarvan Harbour ; Lismore (1474) and Cappoquin (1069) are beautifully situated on the Blackwater. Tramore (1644), on the open sea 7 miles south of Waterford, is a much-frequented watering-place.

Co. Tipperary

A very large county, lying entirely inland, and much diversified by groups of mountains—the Silvermines and Devil's Bit groups in the north, the loftier Galtees (3016 ft.) and Knockmealdowns (2609 ft.), and the

Waterford, from the west

fine, isolated Slievenaman (2564 ft.), in the south. Elsewhere the surface is of the type characteristic of the Central Plain—slightly undulating limestone country, mostly in permanent pasture. The " Golden Vale of Tipperary," famed for its fertility, stretches from

The Old Quay, Clonmel, Co. Tipperary

Fethard westward by Cashel and Tipperary town to Kilmallock. Except for Lough Derg on the Shannon, which flows along the north-western edge of the county, lakes are almost absent. The county is drained by tributaries of the Shannon in the north and by the Suir in the centre and south.

Clonmel (10,209), the chief town, is beautifully situated on the Suir. Lower down the same river is Carrick-on-Suir (5235), and further up are Caher (1930) and

Thurles (4549). Cashel (2813), famous for its ecclesiastical ruins, Tipperary (6645), and Fethard (1473) also lie towards the centre; Nenagh (4776), Roscrea 2182), and Templemore (1791) in the north.

Co. Limerick

The whole northern boundary of Co. Limerick is formed by the Shannon, mostly by its broad, lake-like estuary—" The spacious Shenan spreading like a sea," as Spenser describes it. The greater part of the area, particularly the north, is low, with extensive limestone pasture-lands. Round the other three sides—west, south, and north—the county is fringed with hills, which attain their greatest elevation in the south-east, where the boundary passes over the summit of Galtymore (3015 ft.). As a result of this grouping of the higher grounds, the drainage of the county is all northward across the plain to the Shannon.

Limerick (38,518), a very ancient city, stands on the Shannon at the point where the river becomes tidal, on the site of an important ford ; the original Luimneach or Limnagh stood on King's Island, guarding the ford, and itself safe from sudden attack. In the eighteenth century, before the construction of railways diverted the lines of traffic, this was a very busy town and port ; but, like many of the western towns,

> "Limerick prodigious,
> That stands with quays and bridges,
> And the ships up to the windys
> Of the Shannon shore,"

has now somewhat declined in relative importance ; but it is still a busy place well supplied with railways, and the distributing centre for a very large district.

There is a steamer service down the Shannon to its mouth. The other towns within the county are much smaller : Rathkeale (1705) and Newcastle (2585), both lying towards the west, are the most important.

Co. Clare

For nearly three-quarters of its periphery Clare is bordered by water—by the Atlantic along its extended western side, and by the Shannon and its great estuary on the east and south. The Atlantic coast is bare and mostly cliff-bound, with no shelter for ships between Galway Bay and the Shannon. In. the north, the strange, bare limestone hills of Burren, already described (p. 18), overlook the ocean ; and these naked limestones continue into the centre of the county, where there are many low-lying lakes. Coal-measures, forming bleak, treeless hills, cover much of the west ; the centre is a low-lying plain of limestone ; the east is fertile, and pleasantly diversified with woods and lakes, valleys and hills—the last rising to 1746 ft. in Slieve Bernagh, where the county fronts Lough Derg. The Aran Islands, lying across the entrance of Galway Bay, belong geologically to Clare, being shelves of limestone rock forming a continuation of the limestone beds of Burren ; but politically they belong to Co. Galway, and are dealt with in the Connaught volume of this series.

Ennis, the assize town (5472), stands on the low ground in the centre of the county, on the River Fergus, above the head of its broad, shallow, island-studded estuary. Kilrush (3666) is on the Shannon estuary near its mouth ; a few miles to the west, Kilkee (1688), a favourite seaside resort, faces the open Atlantic. Killaloe (821) is beautifully placed on the Shannon at the foot of Lough Derg, where the river plunges through the interesting gorge referred to on p. 19. It was an important ecclesiastical centre in old days. Ennistymon (1204) and Miltown Malbay (995) are close to the west coast ; Lisdoonvarna (249), towards the north, has mineral springs, and is a well-known health resort.

GEOLOGY

THE rock formations which are met with in Munster belong to the Palæozoic Group. They comprise the following systems, which are arranged in age order, the oldest being below :—

> Carboniferous.
> Old Red Sandstone.
> Silurian.
> Ordovician.

In the earliest or Ordovician period a sea with islands scattered over it occupied the British area. Near the shores sands and muds accumulated to form sandstones and shales. In the clearer waters shell-fish of obsolete types abounded, and from their dead shells were formed bands of limestones. Corals, too, were present in this sea, which goes to prove that our islands were then bathed by warmer waters than those which surround them to-day.

Great volcanic activity prevailed at this time. In Wales and Cumberland, in counties Dublin and Kildare volcanoes existed. In Waterford we have a grand series of volcanic rocks which burst their way through the sea-floor and mingled their lavas and ashes with the sands and muds, causing destruction among the shell-fish and coral polyps. Slates of Ordovician age are found in the vicinity of Waterford.

The Silurian period was a more peaceful time here and in the British area generally, but in the Dingle peninsula the final struggles of these plutonic forces were enacted. At Clogher Head, and along the coast north and south, the Atlantic has laid bare old lavas and ashes that were poured out upon the bottom of the sea. Now and again came paroxysmic eruptions sufficient to blot out of existence the abundant animal life of those waters, but it soon returned, and so we find sediments again forming on top of an old lava flow. In addition to this district already mentioned, Silurian rocks are also found on the plateau between the Commeragh mountains and Portlaw, in the district east of Slievenamann and in the region west of the Galtee mountains. The highlands west and south of the Devil's Bit reveal large areas of Silurian rocks, and we find them abundantly displayed in the Arra and Silvermine mountains in Tipperary and also in the Slieve Bernagh and Slieve Aughty mountains west of the Shannon. In all cases their exposure is due to the removal by denudation of the Old Red Sandstone rocks which rested upon them.

With the beginning of Old Red Sandstone times great crustal movements took place in N.W. Europe, and folds were developed whose axes ran in a north-easterly direction. The sea was thus excluded from the Irish area, and from Britain north of the Bristol Channel. Desert conditions appear to have prevailed on this continental land. Mountains were buried beneath their own detritus, and sands accumulated on desert plains and in

delta, lake or estuary. Red oxide of iron is the characteristic cementing material of most of these accumulations.
In the upper division of the Old Red Sandstone rocks
are yellow sandstones. These in the vicinity of Cork
and at Ballyhale, near Waterford, yield plant remains
possessing a fern-like foliage which were washed down
and embedded in the fine-grained sands.

The mountains and hills of the south of Ireland are
for the most part carved out of Old Red Sandstone
rocks. In Co. Cork they rise towards the west, until
in the moorland on the confines of Kerry west of Gouganebarra they attain a height of over 1500 ft. Farther west
in Kerry are moorlands still higher. The finest groups,
however, of these Old Red Sandstone mountains lie
in the region of the Macgillicuddy's Reeks, and here Carn
Tual rises to 3414 ft., the loftiest point in the island.

Passing towards the east are the Mangerton range,
the Paps, Boggeragh and Nagles mountains, all carved
out of this red rock. North of Lismore are the Knockmealdowns with one dominating peak, whilst the Comeraghs form an Old Red Sandstone plateau with a
steep escarpment on the eastern side, indented at
intervals by river valleys, at the heads of which are
often found basin-shaped hollows or cirques. North
of the Knockmealdowns are the Galtees. Here the
weathering of the horizontally-bedded sandstones has
formed the flat-topped Galteemore. Slievenamuck,
north of this, leads on to another exposure of these
rocks around the Silurian high land, which occupies
most of the north-west of Co. Tipperary. On the east
of this highland is the Devil's Bit mountain, so called
because of the notch from which the Old Red Sandstone
has been entirely removed (possibly by a river in the

latter part of the glacial period), thus making the hill to the south an outlier of the main sandstone mass to the north. The highest point in the Silvermines is composed of Old Red Sandstone; and Keeper Hill is capped by an outlier of this rock. It also occurs in the Arra mountains on the east of the Shannon and in the Slieve Bernagh range in Clare. Farther north a large development of this formation is found in the Slieve Aughty range. In every case the appearance of Old Red Sandstone rocks is due to the weathering of the Carboniferous rocks by which they were originally covered throughout the whole area.

Volcanic rocks of this period consisting of lavas and ashes are met with at Loo Bridge and south of Lough Guitane in Kerry. A little to the south of Limerick is Knockfeerina Hill, which was an old volcanic vent in the latter part of this period.

The Carboniferous Period was heralded in by a gradual sinking of the land surface. The depression probably set in from the south, but finally the sea extended until practically the whole of the country was covered. An old shore line may have existed somewhere among the highlands of Donegal and Mayo, and part of the Leinster chain, the granite of which by this time had been largely denuded of its shaly covering, remained as land for a time, for pebbles of granite are found in the limestone near Dublin.

This sea stretched eastwards through England into the heart of Europe. In it oozes were formed, partly from remains of animals like sea-lilies, which were invested with a skeleton composed of calcareous plates. Shell-fish, too, were numerous, and in the vicinity of the shores or upon shoals, corals multiplied and added their share in the formation of the massive limestones which we find so widely developed throughout the country.

After a lapse of time the mouths of the rivers which entered this sea became silted up; large deltas of sand were formed which stretched out into it as that of the Mississippi does now into the Gulf of Mexico.

In course of time forests grew upon the newly-formed land. The vegetation in these was composed of many strange types. Club mosses, represented to-day by lowly plants found in bogs, grew into tall trees. Likewise did the calamites, which grow in swampy places and were somewhat like our horse-tails. Tree ferns and cycads, reminding us of tropical vegetation, were abundant in the lowlands, while pines clothed the sides of the mountains. These forests flourished and decayed, and, as the ground upon which they grew sank beneath the sea, were covered by sand and clay. Other deltas were afterwards formed on the same spot and forests again occupied them, to be buried in their turn by the next depression. Thus many coal seams separated by beds of sandstones or shale were formed in succession at the same place. To the whole series of these rocks the general name of Coal Measures has been given. It is difficult to find at the present time anything to which we may compare these old forests, though perhaps in the mangrove swamps of Florida we may get a dim idea of the conditions prevailing in the latter part of the Carboniferous period.

Around Limerick and extending south-eastwards for some 20 miles is a large area in which is displayed abundant evidence of volcanic activity during Carboniferous times. The lavas and ashes have resisted the action of the weather better than the limestone which envelops them, and thus they form a series of low hills which are rendered conspicuous because of the flatness of the surrounding country. The old castle of Carrigogunnel, 5 miles west of the city, stands on one of these igneous masses. Caherconlish is another large exposure, whilst about Pallas Green and Herbertstown they are developed in an almost continuous zone.

The Carboniferous rocks may be divided into four groups. Given in order, the earliest being below, they are :

> Coal Measures.
> Millstone Grit.
> Limestone.
> Shale.

The Shale is found commonly at the sides of the valleys in the south of Ireland, and generally as a thin band surrounding the exposures of Old Red Sandstone. In the south of Cork is a large area of Carboniferous Slate which represents a much longer epoch than that in which the Lower Limestone Shale of the rest of the country was formed. With the slates are associated the " Coomhola Grits " which are found well developed on Shehy mountain north-west of Dunmanway.

Limestone occupies the valleys from that of Cloyne northwards. Tongues of this rock extending from the Central Plain envelop the Galtees, one pushing through by Charleville to Mallow, the other reaching round by Caher and Mitchelstown. Six miles east of this latter place are the well-known caves. These were formed by the solution of the limestone, and in them are many beautiful columns made by the coalescence of stalactites suspended from the roof with stalagmites formed on the floor below.

In the northern part of Clare the magnificent terraced mountains of the Burren are carved out of horizontally

Stalactite-Stalagmite Pillar in Cave six miles E. of Mitchelstown, Co. Cork

bedded limestone. This rock is also exposed in a band some 12 miles wide running south through and to the east of Ennis and reaching the Shannon.

South and west of the limestone area are large exposures of Carboniferous sandstone. Perhaps the most striking of these is to be found in the long range of the cliffs of Moher. These vertical cliffs of horizontally bedded sandstone are perhaps the finest in the British Isles. At the northern end, near O'Brien's Tower, one may lie on the edge of the cliff and drop a pebble into the Atlantic 600 ft. below. At Kilkee we have also magnificent cliff scenery, and here some of the surfaces of the sandstones exhibit excellent examples of ripple marks.

Limestone Terraces, Co. Clare

Coal Measures strata are found in North-west Cork, North-east Kerry, and South Clare, whilst in Tipperary there is a small exposure of them about 10 miles south-east of Thurles. These areas are surrounded by rocks of the Millstone Grit series.

After the Coal Measures were formed a great uplift accompanied by folding took place in the north-west of Europe. Our area was greatly affected by this, and the present trend of river valley and upland ridge so conspicuous in the physical features of Munster are due to the unequal denudation of the hard rocks exposed in the crests of the folds and the weaker ones which still remain in the troughs.

A long extended period of denudation now followed,

The Cliffs at Kilkee, Co. Clare

and the Coal Measures that occupied large areas were eventually removed from most of the province.

Very little is known of the subsequent history between this post-Carboniferous upheaval and Glacial times. It is probable, however, that the sea did cover the area during a part of this wide interval and that newer deposits than the Carboniferous rocks were laid down, but of these not the slightest trace remains. All we know is, that before the advent of Glacial times the main features of the topography were much as they are to-day.

One of the most noticeable features of the river system of Cork is the sharp right-angled bend which occurs in each of the three rivers—Blackwater, Lee, and Bandon—in the lower portion of their courses, and the steep-sided gorges through which they have each cut a passage to the sea.

The Blackwater, after bending south at Cappoquin, enters a deep ravine, the sides of which rise to between 300 and 400 ft. Now if a dam 80 ft. high were formed across the river at Dromana, it would, after forming a lake about Cappoquin, make its way to the sea at Dungarvan. Similarly if the east and west passages of the Lee were blocked the river would go along by Midleton to Ballycottin Bay. The Bandon too, under similar circumstances, would find an outlet by the Owenboy valley and enter the sea at Cork Harbour by Carrigaline.

It is evident that the carving of these gorges was begun before the valleys behind had been reduced to anything like their present levels.

Let us now consider events in the light of a theory proposed by Professor Jukes as far back as 1862.

After the formation of the Coal Measures the whole of Munster was affected by forces which elevated the crust and produced folds in the rocks. The new land thus formed was subjected to denudation by the sea, and most of our coal supplies were removed, leaving a gently sloping surface of limestone through which here and there the Old Red Sandstone rocks made their appearance in the crests of the folds or *anticlines* where the limestone had been eaten through. Eventually after another uplift a series of rivers flowed down this sloping surface towards the south. The Brinny brook continued its way along the lower course of the Bandon, the stream of the Glanmire valley came down by Passage West, and the Owenacurra flowed past Midleton and by Passage East and effected a junction with it somewhere in Cork Harbour, the confluent waters going through the harbour entrance to the sea, whilst in the case of the Blackwater the youthful ravines of Dromana and Carnglass formed the channel for a river flowing from the Knockmealdowns.

Continued denudation in the course of time laid bare the sandstone all along the anticlines of the east and west folds, and since the sandstone was more resistant than the limestone which remained in the synclines, the east and west tributary valleys were carved out of the latter rock, which yielded so readily to solution by water containing carbonic acid gas. The western tributaries of the streams increased more rapidly than those flowing from the east, for the slope of the land was in their favour, the higher ground being in the west; and thus it comes about that the original western tributaries now form the main portions of the present-day rivers.

Near Killaloe the Shannon passes through a gorge, the banks of which run up to elevations of 1746 ft. on the western side and 1517 ft. on the eastern, whilst the bed of the river is only 108 ft. above sea level. It is quite certain that the limestone of the plain north of this was much higher than either the Slieve Bernagh or the Arra mountains when the Shannon began its life-work; and that it had power to carve through the more resistant sandstone rocks as rapidly as the lowering of the limestone plain to the north was affected by denudation.

The same reasoning can be applied to the Suir, which leaves the limestone plain and goes through a gorge with sides 250 ft. in height near the city of Waterford.

THE GLACIAL PERIOD

At the beginning of this period the sea stood at approximately the same level as now. The annual snowfall was greater than the heat of summer could melt, and hence an ice-sheet was formed. This ice-sheet appeared much earlier in the north than in the south. Gradually, however, invasions of ice from the great Central Plain and of Irish Sea ice took place, the former finding a way at first through the passes of the hills, but afterwards mounting and overtopping most of them, the latter occupying and riding over the country along the coasts of Waterford and Cork. The highlands of Kerry nursed their own glaciers and these were pushed out in all directions, and finally joined the northern and eastern sheets.

In Cork the striations on the rocks run east-south-east, and these, taken in conjunction with other glacial data, indicate an ice movement in that direction. The sea to the south was probably occupied by ice, else we should expect to find that tongues of ice escaped through such openings as Cork Harbour, but of this there is no evidence.

In Clare the main ice-stream seems to have come from Galway, for boulders of Galway granite are found in the boulder clay of many different localities in this county.

On the shrinkage of the Irish Sea ice, the Cork ice-sheet advanced, and we find south of Youghal red boulder clay overlying the marly marine deposit, showing that there were no intervening interglacial deposits in this district.

The glaciation of the south was of much shorter duration than that of the country farther north. This is not to be wondered at, for Munster appears to have

Roche moutonnée at Loo Bridge, Co. Kerry

lain just inside the margin of the British ice-sheets, and in this connection it may be borne in mind that signs of glaciation are not found in the adjoining island farther south than Bristol and the Thames valley.

The hills in south-east Cork thus emerged at an earlier period than did those of the west, and upon the newly bared surface a copious land drainage was soon established. Glaciers still occupied the valleys however,

m E

and it is to rivers that flowed along the sides of these glaciers that we owe the stratified gravels so common in the Lee valley and elsewhere.

In some cases the earlier courses of the streams were blocked up either with ice or drift, and the diverted streams cut new channels which are now either dry or supplied by insignificant streams.

The time immediately following the Glacial period was one of severe winters, when snows accumulated, giving rise to heavy floods in spring. Under these conditions the sharp V-shaped north and south transverse gorges were excavated, and the materials removed from them were spread out in the form of fans where these gorges open out on the broader eastward valleys. The main rivers, too, carried considerably more water than they do now, and thus they were able to bring down the gravels that are found in such quantity in the lower reaches of the valleys.

As milder conditions came on the glaciers diminished in size and in length. They retreated up the valleys, but this retreat was interrupted repeatedly by periods of rest. These periods are marked by morainic mounds which stretch across the valleys from side to side. In some instances most of the materials of these moraines have been removed by the river and only scattered mounds indicate their former extension. A fine example of a moraine on a small scale is to be seen in the Gap of Dunloe, west of Killarney. Here the large lateral moraine of the east side of the Gap joins up with the terminal moraine lower down, thus forming a horse-shoe embankment in the valley.

Moraines are found in most of the valleys in the Macgillicuddy Reeks district. About Killarney, and in the valley east of this around Lough Guitane, are fine examples, while another fairly well preserved one occurs in the Sheen valley south of Kenmare.

One of the most striking features of a recently glaciated country is the abundance of its lakes. These are formed in various ways. Sometimes they are excavated rock basins filled with water, as in Lough Auger in the Gap of Dunloe ; in other cases they occupy hollows between the surrounding mounds of drift, as in Cork Lough ; or, again, a moraine may block up a valley and a lake be formed behind. There are a very large number of moraine-dammed lakes among the Kerry hills, and the Lakes of Killarney themselves are banked on the north by morainic material. In the southern part of the Comeragh plateau are several lakes of quite a different type, the most noted of these being Lake Coumshingaun. Ascending one of the branches of the Clodiach river we mount a series of moraines with huge blocks of Old Red Sandstone scattered about upon them. Behind the highest and last of these is the lake itself, which is bounded on the farther side by a semi-circular wall of cliff rising sheer from the water's edge. This marks the spot where the remains of a glacier sheltered during the latter part of the glacial epoch. As milder conditions came on the ice melted and formed a lake. This was fed by small streams from the high land behind the cliff and eventually rose to the level of the lowest part of the moraine dam, over which it flowed and easily carved out a bed in the loosely compacted embankment.

Many of these coom, corrie or cirque lakes are found in the mountainous parts of Kerry. Facing the sea, on the northern side of the Dingle peninsula are fine examples,

whilst at the head of the Glenbeigh valley, near Cahersi-
veen is a series of seven—the finest in the British Isles.

In Co. Cork are quite a number of instances of river
diversion. The Bride stream that entered the Lee
valley from the north by the Shandon Gap was blocked
by a stratified gravel deposit. This was probably formed
in a lake at a time when the Lee valley was occupied
by a glacier. After the ice had disappeared this lake
sought an outlet and formed the present ravine known
as Goulding's Glen, at the side of the main obstruction.
The river soon removed the gravels and cut deeply
into the sandstone. Another striking instance occurs
at Tattan's Gorse, about half-way between Watergrasshill
and Midleton. The stream flowing from the north was
blocked by ice or drift at Dooneen Bridge, and a new course
with steep sides 70 ft. high was cut out of sandstone
rock a little to the east, and through this the Leamlara
stream still flows. At Riverstown, in the Glanmire
valley, the Glashaboy stream has been diverted from
its original course by a bank of glacial gravel, and a
passage has been cut through the rock 60 ft. deep
and 200 to 300 yards long.

The stream that flows through the pass of Keimaneigh
could not have cut that famous gorge. More probably
it was rapidly cut out by flood waters consequent
upon the shrinkage of the ice.

Erratics are abundant, especially in the south-west of
Munster. These are blocks, often of great size, that have
been carried from their place of origin by ice. When
they occupy precarious positions they are termed perched
blocks. At Cloughlowrish Bridge, in Co. Waterford, is
an erratic of Old Red Sandstone resting upon an igneous
rock. Near Kenmare is another of sandstone resting

upon a limestone surface. The limestone has been artificially cut away all round at a remote period, so that the large erratic now rests on a slender pedestal. On Knockbrack mountain are a large number of them, and about Glengariff and westwards towards Adrigole they are perched in all kinds of positions.

Perched Block, Co. Kerry

At the end of the Mer de Glace, near Chamounix, are rocks which present a smooth and polished surface and on which striations are also observable. The smoothing has been effected by the sand which the ice contained in its base, and the striations are due to the chiselling action of fragments of rocks held as in a vice by the glacier as it moved forward.

One of the surest forms of evidence concerning the motion of glaciers is to be found in such smoothed surfaces of rock upon which are striations more or less deeply incised. Some of these begin as fine lines and increase in thickness until they come to an abrupt termination. In this case the striation becomes coarser in the direction in which the glacier was moving.

Sometimes two or more sets of striations are observable; in Cork and Kerry we have many examples of this. Thus at the head of the Slaheny valley is a rock surface with two distinct sets of striations and a third somewhat less distinctly marked. The chief glaciation has produced ridges and furrows running S. 33° E., while a later set of striations runs E. 10° S. These later striations are found on only one side of the smoothed ridges, and consequently we assume that the striated side of the ridge was that opposed to the motion of the latter glacier.

While, as already stated, the general course of the glaciers in Cork was east-south-east, they nevertheless followed valleys which deviated from this direction. Thus a part of the glacier from the Roughty valley, east of Kilgarvan, went N.E. towards Ballyvourney, while another part kept on down the valley of the Toon to Macroom. The striations show that meanders of the valleys were also followed fairly closely by the ice, or that a differential movement existed in different parts of the same ice mass.

The gravels have been already referred to as being formed by floods consequent upon the breaking up of the ice-sheet. They are found at different levels. The higher ones were formed by the earlier floods at a time when the hill-tops were stripped of ice, the lower ones later on when ice occupied only the lower parts of the valleys. Behind the village of Watergrasshill, at a height of 600 ft., are representatives of these earlier flood gravels, while in the Lee valley, about Cork and also about Midleton, are later deposits.

Eskers, or low winding ridges formed of water-worn

Glaciated rock surface, Co. Cork

and stratified material, are not developed in such fine proportions in Munster as in King's County, Westmeath, or Tyrone. A small one occurs at Dooneen Bridge, 5 miles south-west of Limerick, and another at Kenmare, just below the Great Southern Railway Hotel. These seem to have been formed where sub-glacial streams heavily charged with sediment and flowing in ice tunnels reached the quiet waters of a lake or estuary.

The gravels which were spread out on the bottom of the valleys by the floods during the time of recession of the ice have since been cut into by the rivers, and terraces have been formed marking the different successive flood levels. Good examples of these are seen in the Lee valley at Inniscarra and Carrigrohane, six and

Terraces at Inniscarra on the River Lee

three miles respectively west of Cork. In these the highest terraces give approximately the level of the old gravel-covered plain. As the river deepened its bed new flood terraces were formed at successively lower levels.

At many points along the southern coast-line from Carnsore Point to Baltimore portions of an old shore-line have been traced. Where well preserved, as at Myrtleville, a little west of the entrance to Cork Harbour, it consists of a tidal platform rising from present mean-tide level on the outer edge to a few feet above high-tide mark on the landward side. Upon this we get, amongst other deposits, one of boulder clay.

Now if we consider that the gorges of the Lee at Passage East and Passage West were formed by the cutting action of the river when the land stood at a higher level, we must admit, on the testimony of the raised beaches, that a pre-glacial subsidence admitted the sea to the lower parts of the rivers and formed those long inlets or rias, examples of which we have in Waterford and Cork Harbours and in the long inlets which form such striking features of the coast-line of Cork and Kerry. As this old beach corresponds with those on the opposite side of St George's Channel, it is fair to assume that Ireland was separated from England before the advent of the glacial period, though during a part of this period a land-connection may have been re-established. Be that as it may, we have at the present time the sea level very nearly restored to the old position which it occupied before the coming of the ice age.

SOILS

The loose ice-borne material or drift, from which is derived most of the soils of the cultivated lands, is throughout most of the province similar to the debris of the rocks upon which it rests, and thus there is little difference between the derived soils in the two cases. An exception occurs in the soils at the head of Bantry Bay. These are greatly enriched by the limestone boulder clay. A similar enrichment is found to follow the presence of this type of boulder clay in the vicinity of the Silurian hills of Tipperary, whilst the Vale of

Aherlow and the Golden Vale of Limerick owe their wealth of soil to the large proportion of limestone and volcanic rocks in the mixed materials of the drifts in those places.

In North Clare we have a large area of bare limestone in which meteoric agencies have carved out the magnificent natural terraces of the Burren. Drifts occur in the valleys and are largely made up of limestone detritus, with some pebbles and blocks of Galway granite. Further south limestone blocks are associated with sandstone and shale in the drift.

The drift covering about Listowel and Tralee Bay is made up largely of limestone debris, but in the centre of Kerry grits and shales are the principal constituents.

In south-west Kerry moraines are common in the gaps of the mountains, and in the vicinity of Killarney the limestone is overspread with drift and moraines, which are alike formed of grits and shales from the Old Red Sandstone country to the south.

MINES, MINERALS, AND QUARRIES

In south-west Cork a number of veins of copper ore have been found. The ore is chiefly Copper Pyrites ($CuFeS_2$). In the past a large quantity of this ore has been taken out, more particularly in the district west of Berehaven. At Ross Island, Killarney, and at Ardtully, in the Kenmare valley, copper mining has been carried on. Other places extensively worked in the past are Knockmahon and Bunmahon, west of Annestown, Co. Waterford. In Tipperary copper ore occurs at Lackamore.

At Duneen Bay, near Clonakilty, there occurs a rich

vein of Barytes. This mineral is also found at Skull. In both places the ore is worked.

Lead mines have been worked in the Silvermines district, near Nenagh, also at Tulla in Clare and at Rooska, near Bantry. Galena (PbS.) is the chief ore.

Pyrolusite (MnO_2), has been obtained in the vicinity of Glandore, Co. Cork, and the zinc ore, Calamine, occurs in the Silvermines district, Co. Tipperary.

Limestone is used very largely as a building stone all over the province. In the south it has been subjected to great earth-pressures and has developed cleavage. This takes away from its value as a building stone. Nevertheless stones of large size suitable for columns have been quarried at Ballintemple, and these have been employed in the building of the Courthouse and Savings Bank in the city of Cork. As the stone weathers, the fossils, so difficult to determine in freshly fractured specimens, stand out in relief owing to their superior hardness, and this gives it a delicate veined appearance which adds greatly to the beauty of the stone.

Red marble is found at Little Island, Fermoy, Midleton in Co. Cork, and Castleisland in Co. Kerry. The colour is due to the infiltration of iron oxide. Good examples of the use of Cork marbles in interior decoration can be seen in St Finbarre's Cathedral and in the entrance hall of the new Technical School, Cork ; and of Castleisland marble in the Honan Chapel, University College. Grey marble is found at Mitchelstown.

Limestone is burnt in many places, and the lime obtained is used for building, whitewash, and agricultural purposes. The old style of kiln is being superseded by one which has a larger " eye " or opening at the base, and this is directed so as to catch the prevailing S.W. winds, instead of facing the east as in the older types. The impurities in some of the limestones render them more effective for agricultural purposes than as a wash. Dolomitisation (the replacing of Calcium by Magnesium) has occurred in some of the limestones around Cork, and from this altered rock Magnesia was formerly made. It is now extracted from sea water at Little Island.

Coal Measures occur in N.W. Cork, N.E. Kerry, W. Limerick, and S. Clare. The seams are anthracitic but thin, and are of little commercial importance. A more flourishing coal-field is that of Slieve Ardagh, in Tipperary. This is worked, and has a yearly output of eight thousand five hundred tons.

Owing to the extensive use of limestone in building and the scarcity of good brick clays, the brick-making industry is of less importance in the south than in the north of Ireland. A stiff white clay occurs in places over the limestone drift. Brick clay also occurs along the River Fergus, and at Listowel, Tralee, Newcastle West, Limerick, Nenagh, and near Thurles, also at Youghal, Monard, Belvelly, and Ballinphelic. At the last named place red tiles, chimney-pots, and other articles in earthenware were manufactured until quite recently. The products were conveyed to Ballinhassig station, 4 miles distant, by trolleys running on an overhead cable. Potter's clay is found near Killenaule, Co. Tipperary, and at Youghal in addition to brick works is a small pottery industry.

Some of the old slates formerly used in Cork were obtained in the county, and at present some quarries are being worked. At Killaloe and Portree, near Nenagh, the output is much greater. The slate quarries near Carrick-on-Suir yield a small supply.

In the absence of igneous rocks, which are poorly represented in Munster except in the vicinity of Limerick, limestone, sandstone, and slate are used as road metal. Of these limestone and slate are used in the valleys and sandstone on the higher ground. Partly on account of their situation roads made from the latter rock are better than those of the valleys. Bands of " Coomhola Grit " occur in the Carboniferous shale series, and these provide a better material than any of the others.

Experiments on road metals have been conducted by the Engineering Department at University College, Cork. The instrument employed is a rattler or drum, into which a certain weight of broken stone of standard size as used on the roads is introduced, together with a number of small cubical blocks of iron. These are rotated for 50 minutes and the amount of debris, consisting of chippings and dust, determined. In these tests southern limestones come out badly, but some of the Coomhola sandstones give much better results, and are intermediate in quality between the limestones and well-known igneous road metals, such as Penmanmawr rock. One of the best of these grits is quarried at Killeady, near Kinsale. Paving setts are made in the Longstone quarries near Limerick, and these have superseded those imported from Wales and Arklow, which were formerly used in that city. Flags are quarried at Doonagoore and other places in the county of Clare.

BOTANY

THE province of Munster is much diversified as to surface. As we pass southward out of the Central Plain the continuity of the limestone which prevails there is more and more broken up by high ridges running east and west or north-east and south-west. The extensive folding which took place in post-Carboniferous times, and subsequent denudation, have laid bare the underlying Devonian and Silurian rocks, which now form the hill-ranges, while on the lower grounds the limestone still persists. We have thus the same broad contrast which we find in Connaught—the grassy plain with a calcicole flora, and the heathery hills with a calcifuge vegetation. In Clare and North Kerry there are also large areas of Coal-measures resting on the limestone, and usually supplying a heavy lime-free soil. In the south-west, where great mountain-ribs, projecting far into the Atlantic, alternate with deep troughs in which the limestone still lingers, the mildness and dampness which characterise the Irish climate reach their maximum, and there is a remarkable fauna and flora, characterised by the occurrence of many species, chiefly plants, which find here their most northerly known station. And mixed incongruously with these we find, as elsewhere in Ireland, other species which are of high northern distribution. The interesting question as to the origin of these elements in the flora and fauna has been touched on in the "Ireland" volume of this series, and need not be reviewed here.

Pinguicula grandiflora

Of the interesting group of species referred to in the last paragraph the most conspicuous are certain flowering plants, namely : *Arbutus Unedo*, the Strawberry Tree (found in the Killarney district, S.W. France, Pyrenees, Mediterranean), *Saxifraga umbrosa* and *S. Geum* (S. to W. or N.W. Ireland, Pyrenean region), *Pinguicula grandiflora* (S.W. Ireland, Pyrenean region, Alps), *Euphorbia hiberna* (S. to N.W. Ireland, Devon, Pyrenean region), *Sibthorpia europæa* (Kerry, S.W. England, France, Spain, Portugal), *Spiranthes Romanzoffiana* (Cork, N. Ireland, Kamtschatka, northern N. America), *Simethis bicolor* (Kerry, Dorset, Spanish Peninsula and West Mediterranean), *Sisyrinchium angustifolium* (S.W. to N.W. Ireland, northern N. America), *Eriocaulon septangulare* (S.W. to N.W. Ireland, Skye, N. America). Nowhere else in Europe do we find such an interesting and puzzling mixture of southern and northern plants living together so far removed from their centre of distribution.

We may now consider in greater detail the flora of some selected areas within the province.

Macgillicuddy's Reeks

" The Reeks " (ricks) are the finest as well as the loftiest mountain range in Ireland. The highest point (Carrantuohill) reaches 3414 ft., and along the main ridge for several miles an elevation of over 3000 ft. is maintained. Composed of massive slates and sandstones of Devonian age, the numerous lofty precipices are formed of hard rock, suitable for plant life and safe for the climber. A number of tarns lie among the hills, surrounded by magnificent cirques. As elsewhere in Ireland, the number of alpine plants which occur is limited, and is not in proportion to the large amount of suitable ground. The Highland type Phanerogams

Strawberry Tree (*Arbutus Unedo*) at the **Upper Lake of Killarney**

of the range are *Draba incana, Sedum roseum, Saxifraga stellaris, Hieracium anglicum, Oxyria digyna,*

m F

Salix herbacea, Carex rigida. They are accompanied on the high grounds by *Armeria maritima* and *Cochlearia alpina.* *Silene maritima* occurs lower down, far from the sea. The tarns yield *Subularia aquatica, Elatine hexandra, Lobelia Dortmanna, Sparganium minimum,* etc. Many of the interesting plants of the Kerry lowlands creep up the flanks of the hills. *Saxifraga umbrosa* is, as usual, found at all elevations. Lower down we get *S. Geum, S. hirsuta, Carum verticillatum, Bartsia viscosa, Utricularia Bremii, Pinguicula grandiflora, Euphorbia hiberna.*

The Killarney Lakes

The town of Killarney, and the large Lower Lake, lie in an east-and-west limestone trough. Northward the ground rises gently into low, boggy, barren hills formed of Coal-measures. Southward the ground rises abruptly from the very shore of the lake into the beautiful and lofty mountains of Old Red Sandstone for which the place is famous. The Upper Lake, which is small and narrow, lies in a mountainous north-and-south valley which penetrates into the hills. There is a striking contrast of both scenery and flora—the low limestones with their grass, tillage, and calcicole plants on the one hand, the high heathery hills on the other. The limestone lies bare, often fantastically carved by water, along the shores and islands of the Lower Lake. In this area, in the woods, on the shores, or in the water, we find :

Subularia aquatica	R. Frangula
Elatine hexandra	Rubia peregrina
Rhamnus catharticus	Galium boreale

G. sylvestre
Carum verticillatum
Lobelia Dortmanna
Wahlenbergia hederacea
Arbutus Unedo
Microcala filiformis
Bartsia viscosa

Monotropa Hypopithys
Utricularia neglecta
Cephalanthera ensifolia
Naias flexilis
Carex Bœnninghausiana
Lastrea Thelypteris
Isoëtes lacustris

The Upper Lake and its neighbourhood, with its dense woods, and reefs and cliffs of Old Red Sandstone, harbours a calcifuge flora of very luxuriant growth, the mildness and dampness of the climate being well shown by the sheets of Filmy Ferns (*Hymenophyllum tunbridgense* and *H. unilaterale*) which clothe the rocks and tree-stems. These woods are the headquarters of the Arbutus, perhaps the most interesting member of the Killarney flora (but it grows also on the limestone islands of the Lower Lake, as shown by the preceding list). It is accompanied here by Oak (Quercus), Birch (Betula), Holly (Ilex), Mountain Ash, *Pyrus Aucuparia*, etc. Most of the other interesting plants of the Upper Lake occur on rocks or on the lake shores :

Subularia aquatica
Elatine hexandra
Saxifraga umbrosa
S. Geum
Pinguicula grandiflora

Euphorbia hiberna
Juncus tenuis
Asplenium Adiantum-
    nigrum, *var.* acutum
Pilularia globulifera

Not far from the Killarney area the rare and handsome Sea Pea (*Lathyrus maritimus*) has its only Irish station at Castlemaine Bay.

Cork

The most striking feature of the botany of the neighbourhood of Cork city is the number and profusion of plants which have escaped from cultivation and are now naturalised. Most of these are of South European distribution. They include *Sedum album, Centranthus ruber, Senecio squalidus* and the hybrid *S. squalidus × vulgaris* (all abundant on walls), *Hypericum hircinum* (Glanmire), *Symphytum tuberosum* (Blackrock), *Erinus alpinus* (Douglas, Blackrock, etc.), *Linaria viscida* (Tivoli, etc.), *Stratiotes aloides* (Ballyphehane bog), *Barbarea præcox, Diplotaxis muralis,* and *Mercurialis annua.* Among the native plants, one of the most interesting is the Irish Spurge, *Euphorbia hiberna,* already referred to ; *Geranium rotundifolium, Pimpinella magna, Rosa micrantha, Carduus nutans, Orobanche Hederæ, Ceratophyllum demersum, Festuca sylvatica.*

The Burren Limestones

The areas of bare limestone which form a characteristic feature of certain tracts, especially in Clare and Galway, harbour one of the most remarkable floras to be found in Ireland. This formation and its accompanying vegetation attain their most striking expression on the hills of the Burren district in northern Clare. Here, over miles of hill and valley, nothing but bare grey rock is to be seen, its innumerable joints worn by weather into a criss-cross of deep fissures which harbour a luxuriant vegetation. This naked ground descends the hills, sweeping down on the southward into central Clare, and on the north surrounding the head of Galway Bay and fringing Lough Corrib and Lough

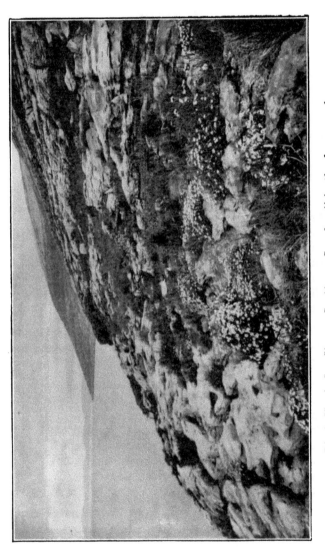

Black Head, Co. Clare. *Saxifraga Sternbergii* in the foreground

Mask, only ceasing at Lough Carra in Mayo. Seaward it occupies in most pronounced form the Aran Islands. Its flora is distinct from that of any other tract in Ireland, being remarkable both for the great abundance of certain plants which usually are locally and sparingly distributed, and for the occurrence, often also in great profusion, of many rare plants, usually of distinctly southern or northern type. A list of the abundant species which immediately impress the eye, and one or other of which in places form the bulk of the vegetation, will include :

Arenaria verna	Asperula cynanchica
Geranium sanguineum	Arctostaphylos Uva-ursi
Rubus saxatilis	Gentiana verna
Dryas octopetala	Euphrasia Salisburgensis
Saxifraga hypnoides	Sesleria cœrulea
Rubia peregrina	Scolopendrium vulgare
Galium sylvestre	Ceterach officinarum

Among other species which are less widespread, though many of them attain an abundant development locally, are :

Helianthemum vineale	Ajuga pyramidalis
Viola stagnina	Taxus baccata
Spiræa Filipendula	Juniperus nana
Potentilla fruticosa	Spiranthes autumnalis
Saxifraga Sternbergii	Epipactis atro-rubens
Galium boreale	Ophrys muscifera
Pyrola media	Neotinea intacta
Orobanche rubra	Adiantum Capillus-Veneris

It will be observed that in spite of an extraordinary mixture of types, the dominant note of this assemblage is alpine-arctic. Sheets of the Dryas, Arctostaphylos, Gentian, and Sesleria cover the ground, all descending to sea-level, and this in a mild area where frost and snow are very rare. Growing with these we find such southern types as *Neotinea intacta* and *Adiantum Capillus-Veneris*, neither of them known elsewhere from so high a latitude, the first having its nearest station in the Mediterranean, the other being a southern species of very wide range. No such extraordinary assemblage of plants is to be found elsewhere in the British Isles.

The Galtees

This fine mountain group, lying mostly in Tipperary, rises to over 3000 ft. (Galtymore, 3015 ft.). They are formed of Silurian and Devonian rocks, and on the northern slope present a very impressive appearance, with numerous lofty precipices overhanging deep tarns. Botanical interest centres on these northern cliff-ranges. Here *Arabis petræa* has one of its two Irish stations, the other being in Glenade, in Co. Leitrim. *Saxifraga umbrosa* flourishes also, finding here its south-eastern limit in Ireland. Other mountain plants which occur are *Meconopsis cambrica, Cochlearia alpina, Sedum roseum, Saxifraga stellaris, S. sponhemica, S. Sternbergii, Saussurea alpina, Hieracium anglicum, Vaccinium Vitis-Idæa, Oxyria digyna, Salix herbacea.* The profusion in which many of these grow on some of the precipices, as on the cliffs over Lough Muskry, compensates for the smallness of their number, and is a striking feature of the botany of the range. The flora of the waters of the lakes is, on the contrary, exceedingly poor.

The Shannon Estuary

The Shannon becomes tidal at Limerick, and, widening into a great estuary, enters the Atlantic 60 miles further on, its mouth being 10 miles wide. The upper reaches are river-like and muddy. Here *Scirpus triqueter* grows in abundance, a very rare plant, unknown elsewhere in Ireland, and in England found only in three southern estuaries. It is accompanied by *Nasturtium sylvestre, Cochlearia anglica, Typha angustifolia* (all very local in Ireland), *Scirpus Tabernæmontani, S. maritimus* and *Phragmites communis.* The adjoining marshy meadows yield *Allium vineale, Leucojum æstivum, Carex riparia, Hordeum secalinum,* and other plants in abundance. The middle parts of the estuary are island-studded, with gravelly or muddy shores. Here we find quantities of *Glyceria festucæformis,* a Mediterranean grass elsewhere known only from Co. Down, and *G. Foucaudi,* found elsewhere only in S.E. England and France ; also such plants as *Apium graveolens, Œnanthe Lachenalii, Artemisia maritima, Statice rariflora, Beta maritima.* The lower part of the estuary assumes the form of an open sea-inlet with rocky and sandy shores, yielding *Glaucium flavum, Raphanus maritimus, Spergularia rupestris, Crithmum maritimum, Euphorbia portlandica,* and other species of similar habitat.

Lough Derg

Lough Derg is the lower of the two great lake-like expansions of the Shannon, the other, Lough Ree, lying further up the river. Save at its southern end, where the lake is embosomed in hills of Silurian slate, the

winding shores are formed of low-lying limestones, and
the numerous islands are composed of the same rock.
Botanical interest centres on the low, uncultivated islets
and reefs, and on the sloping, stony shores.   Here a
peculiar flora is developed, as the following list of
abundant plants will show :

Rhamnus catharticus	Hieracium umbellatum
Hypericum perforatum	Lysimachia vulgaris
Geranium sanguineum	Samolus Valerandi
Rubus cæsius	Erythræa Centaureum
Rosa spinosissima	Chlora perfoliata
Parnassia palustris	Gentiana Amarella
Viburnum Opulus	Lycopus europæus
Galium boreale	Teucrium Scordium
Eupatorium cannabinum	Juniperus communis
Solidago Virgaurea	Schœnus nigricans
Antennaria dioica	Sesleria cœrulea
Carlina vulgaris	Selaginella selaginoides
Cnicus pratensis	

The rarest plant of the lake shores is *Inula salicina,*
which occurs in many places.   Although this species
ranges widely in Europe and Asia, it is unknown elsewhere in the British Isles.   And other rare plants are the
American *Sisyrinchium angustifolium,* which grow in
several places, being abundant along the Woodford river.

Among bryologists, the name of Killarney is famous
as the home of a wonderfully rich moss flora, rich not
only in rare species, but on account of the delightful
profusion and luxuriance in which many of them grow.
The neighbourhood of Glengariff, lying in Co. Cork,
20 miles to the southward, and like Killarney a sheltered,

richly-wooded spot, repeats in some degree the flora of the former place, and when other portions of the remarkably mild, damp valleys of Kerry and West Cork come to be well explored, no doubt fresh stations for many of the Killarney rarities will be found.

Among the most interesting mosses of this south-western district (Kerry and Cork) are: *Trichostomum hibernicum* (not known anywhere else), *Daltonia splachnoides* (Co. Dublin is the only other station in the British Isles), *Leptodontium recurvifolium, Trichostomum fragile, Barbula Hornschuchiana, Ulota Ludwigii, U. calvescens, Œdipodium Griffithianum, Philonotis Wilsoni* (elsewhere in the British Isles in Merioneth and Forfar only), *P. rigida, P. seriata, Webera Tozeri, Ditrichum tortile, Campylopus Schimperi, C. Shawii* (elsewhere in the British Isles known from the Hebrides alone), *C. introflexus* (unknown elsewhere in Ireland : in Great Britain in N. Wales only), *Dicranum flagellare, Fissidens polyphyllus, Campylostelium saxicola, Bryum affine, B. Mildeanum, Sematophyllum demissum* (in Ireland only here ; N. Wales ; Cumberland), *S. micans* (also unknown elsewhere in Ireland ; in Great Britain occurs in Cumberland and the West Highlands), and *Hypnum hamulosum.*

The following may be mentioned also : *Tortula gracilis* (Limerick), *Dicranum schisti* (S. Tipperary), *Bryum Duvalii* (Waterford, only Irish station), the beautiful *Hookeria lætevirens* (confined in Great Britain to Kerry, Cork, Waterford, and Cornwall, with a tropical range abroad), and the calcicole *Eurhynchium striatulum* (Kerry and Limerick).

The south-west of Ireland, and the county of Kerry

in particular. is the richest and most interesting ground for hepatics to be found in the British Isles. This is mainly the result of the extremely mild, moist conditions which prevail there, and the rarest species which occur, if they are found elsewhere at all, belong to countries to the southward. Some of these are unknown elsewhere : others are found nowhere else in the British Isles ; many others, again, have here their only Irish station. Some of the species range up the west coast, and a few of these reappear in western Scotland. Some of the rarest species occur in extraordinary abundance.

Among the greatest treasures of the district are : *Cephalozia hibernica* (Killarney only), *Plagiochila ambagiosa* (Bantry), *Lejeunea flava* (Killarney), *L. Holtii* and *L. diversiloba* (several Kerry stations), *Radula Holtii* and *Bazzania Pearsoni* (Killarney and West Mayo). Other species which find here their only Irish station are : *Lepidozia Pearsoni* (Brandon Mountain), *Fossombronia Dumortieri* (Farranfore), *Anthoceros lævis* (Ventry), *Prionolobus Turneri* (Bantry and Killarney), and *Madotheca Porella* (Cork and Kerry, various stations). The beautiful *Scapania nimbosa* is recorded from Brandon in Kerry and Slievemore in Mayo.

Among many other very rare species which occur may be mentioned *Radula Carringtonii, R. voluta, Scapania ornithopodioides, Mastigophora Woodsii, Pedinophyllum interruptum, Cephalozia leucantha, Lophocolea fragrans, Leptoscyphus cuneifolius, Acrobolbus Wilsonii, Haplomitrium Hookeri, Petalophyllum Ralfsii, Pallavicinia Lyellii, Dumortiera hirsuta.* The profusion and luxuriance of liverworts in the sheltered parts of Kerry and West Cork is very remarkable, and is matched by the profuse growth of mosses and of such ferns as the

Hymenophyllums, which clothe every rock and tree. The remaining portions of Munster, while possessing a varied flora, offer nothing to compare with that of the south-west.

ZOOLOGY

KERRY now possesses the only remnant of the herds of Red Deer (*Cervus elaphus*) that were once so wide-spread in Ireland. The Otter (*Lutra vulgaris*), Badger (*Meles taxus*), Fox (*Canis vulpes*), and Alpine Hare (*Lepus variabilis*), are widely spread ; also the Irish form of the Stoat (*Putorius hibernicus*). The Pine Marten (*Mustela martes*) still occurs occasionally. The Lesser Horse-shoe Bat (*Rhinolophus hipposideros*) has in Kerry the southern limit of its restricted Irish range, which extends thence to Galway. The Great Grey Seal (*Halichœrus grypus*) is a familiar sight along the wilder parts of the coast.

In Munster we find in the north extensive marshes, lakes, and bogs, the breeding-place of many swimming and wading birds. In South Tipperary and Waterford there are high hills with cliff ranges, and cliffs again on the Waterford coast. West Cork and Kerry offer an alternation of wooded valleys and high heathery mountains. The coast of Kerry is extremely broken, with numerous outlying islands, a safe breeding-ground for many species. It will thus be seen that the conditions offered to bird-life are extremely varied.

Of the lakes, by far the most considerable is Lough Derg on the Shannon, which lies mostly in Munster. Its bays and islets support a large bird population in the breeding season, including Common Sandpipers, *Totanus hypoleucus* ; Redshanks, *T. calidris* ; Ringed Plovers, *Ægialitis hiaticola* ; Common Terns, *Sterna fluviatilis* ; Black-headed Gulls, *Larus ridibundus* ; Lesser Black-backed Gulls, *L. fuscus* ; Red-breasted Mergansers, *Mergus serrator* ; Tufted Ducks, *Fuligula cristata* ; Shovellers, *Spatula clypeata* ; and Great Crested Grebes, *Podicipes cristatus*. These species, in greater or less number, constitute the fauna of most of the lakes of the province.

On the mountains the Raven, *Corvus corax*; Peregrine, *Falco peregrinus*; and Merlin, *F. æsalon*, are familiar residents ; Curlew, *Numenius arquata*, and Golden Plover, *Charadrius pluvialis*, nest on the lonely moors. The Ring Ouzel, *Turdus torquatus*, and numbers of Stonechats, *Pratincola rubicola*, and Wheatears, *Saxicola œnanthe*, haunt the heaths ; and Grey Wagtails, *Motacilla melanope*, and Dippers, *Cinclus aquaticus*, are familiar denizens of the streams.

On lowland bogs the Lesser Black-backed Gull, *Larus fuscus*, and Black-headed Gull, *L. ridibundus*, have large colonies. The Nightjar, *Caprimulgus europæus*, is more abundant in Munster than elsewhere in Ireland. Among the larger birds which have recently vanished, or are on the point of extinction, are the Golden Eagle, *Aquila chrysaëtus* (extinct), White-tailed Eagle, *Haliaëtus albicilla*, and Marsh Harrier, *Circus æruginosus*. The Hen Harrier, *C. cyaneus*, still breeds among the mountains.

On the coasts and rocky islands there are great colonies of certain gregarious species : Guillemots, *Uria troile* ; Razorbills, *Alca torda* ; Puffins, *Fratercula arctica* ; Kittiwakes, *Rissa tridactyla*, and so on.

In lesser numbers we find the Manx Shearwater,

Puffinus anglorum (abundant on the Skelligs, rarer elsewhere) ; Black Guillemot, *U. grylle* ; Chough, *Pyrrhocorax graculus* (still abundant in remote places) ; Hooded Çrow, *Corvus cornix* ; Storm Petrel, *Procellaria pelagica,* which breeds in numbers on the Kerry coast. One of the rarest breeders is Leach's Fork-tailed Petrel, *Oceanodroma leucorrhoa,* of which a few eggs have been obtained on the Blasket Islands. The noblest and most interesting of the marine breeding birds of Munster is the Gannet, *Sula bassana.* It nests in only four spots in the British Isles, and of these two are situated off the Munster coast—the Bull Rock in Cork and the Little Skellig in Kerry. On each rock there is a large colony. The most recent accession to the list of breeding birds is the Fulmar, *Fulmarus glacialis,* which has lately established itself. The breeding of the Common Gull, *Larus canus,* is interesting, the Kerry colonies being the most southern in Western Europe.

Among the inland breeding birds which haunt the woodlands are the Blackcap, *Silvia atricapilla* ; Garden Warbler, *S. hortensis* (very local) ; Golden-crested Wren, *Regulus cristatus* (common) ; Crossbill, *Loxia curvirostra* (local) ; Siskin, *Carduelis spinus* ; Tree-Creeper, *Certhia familiaris* ; Long-eared Owl, *Asio otus* ; and Heron, *Ardea cinerea.* As elsewhere in Ireland, the Woodcock, *Scolopax rusticula,* has largely increased as a breeding species. Though the Turtle Dove, *Turtur communis,* is frequently seen in summer, the nest has not so far been discovered.

In winter the fauna of the fields and woods is swelled by the arrival from the east of vast flocks of such birds as Song-Thrushes, *Turdus musicus* ; Blackbirds, *T. merula* ; Fieldfares, *T. pilaris* ; Redwings, *T. iliacus* ;

Starlings, *Sturnus vulgaris* ; Skylarks, *Alauda arvensis* ; Meadow-Pipits, *Anthus pratensis* ; and Chaffinches, *Fringilla cœlebs*.

Among the birds which are known to have spread or to be spreading in the district are the Shoveller, *Spatula clypeata* ; Tufted Duck, *Fuligula cristata*, and Woodcock, *Scolopax rusticula*, all of which have largely increased as breeding species ; the Stock-Dove, *Columba œnas*, a recent arrival in Ireland ; the Missel-Thrush, *Turdus viscivorus*, which seems to have arrived only a little over a century ago ; and the Magpie, *Pica rustica*, first observed in Ireland near the end of the seventeenth century.

The Woodlark, *Alauda arborea*, formerly known to nest in Cork and Waterford, has apparently ceased breeding here, as elsewhere in Ireland, and the Quail, *Coturnix communis*, formerly abundant, is now almost unknown.

Of rare stragglers to Ireland, quite a number have been taken in the province, many of them at island light-stations, others on the mainland. Munster can claim the only Irish records for the following species : Melodious Warbler, *Hypolais polyglotta* (Old Head of Kinsale) ; Yellow-browed Warbler, *Phylloscopus superciliosus* (Tearaght light-station) ; Rufous Warbler, *Aëdon galactodes* (Old Head of Kinsale) ; Griffon Vulture, *Gyps fulvus*, and Spotted Eagle, *Aquila maculata* (both Co. Cork) ; Red-crested Pochard, *Netta rufina* (Tralee, Co. Kerry) ; Great Bustard, *Otis tarda* (two near Thurles, Co. Tipperary) ; Baillon's Crake, *Porzana Bailloni* (one at Youghal and one at Tramore) ; Temminck's Stint, *Tringa Temmincki* (Tralee); Little Dusky Shearwater, *Puffinus assimilis* (Bull Rock, Co. Cork).

Near the mouth of Waterford Harbour, in May 1834, the last specimen of the Great Auk, *Alca impennis*, seen in the British Isles was taken in a landing-net by a fisherman named Kirby. It lived in captivity for four months, and the mounted skin is preserved in Trinity College, Dublin. The fact that bones of this bird have been obtained in some numbers in kitchen-middens in Waterford, Clare, and Antrim points to the conclusion that it was an article of food among the prehistoric people in Ireland.

The only Irish reptile, the Viviparous Lizard (*Lacerta vivipara*), is frequent. The little Natterjack Toad (*Bufo calamita*) is in Ireland confined to a limited area in Co. Kerry, where it is abundant. Co. Waterford boasts the record of the " first Frog " (*Rana temporaria*) seen in Ireland—the authority being Giraldus Cambrensis, and the date about 1187. A later, more circumstantial account of the introduction of this amphibian places the date at 1699, and the venue at Trinity College Park, Dublin. But the occurrence of Frog remains in the deposits found in several Irish caves would seem to show that this animal is an old native of the country. The Common Newt (*Molge vulgaris*) is the only other amphibian occurring in the area.

Ireland is comparatively poor in fresh-water fishes ; almost all of those found in the country occur in Munster. Salmon, *Salmo salar*, are abundant, and the Salmon fisheries are valuable. The Sea-Trout, *S. trutta* and *S. cambricus*, and the Common Trout, *S. fario*, in its various forms (*estuarius*, *stomachicus*, and *ferox*), also abound. Of the Charrs, *S. Colei* is found in Lough Currane. Two other forms, lately described, occur in Kerry—*S. fimbriatus* in Lough Coomasaharn, and *S. obtusus* in Kill Lough and Lough Acoose. Both are so far unknown outside Ireland. The endemic Shannon Pollan, *Coregonus elegans*, is found in Lough Derg. The Allis Shad, *Clupea alosa*, is frequent; the Twaite Shad, *C. finta*, has been taken in the Lakes of Killarney and in the Blackwater. The Dace, *Leuciscus vulgaris*, has its only known Irish station in the lower reaches of the Blackwater. The remaining fishes occurring in the province do not need special comment.

The most interesting species in the molluskan fauna of Munster is undoubtedly the " Kerry Slug," *Geomalacus maculosus*. It is abundant over a considerable area of South Kerry and West Cork, and in damp weather may be seen crawling over the rocks and feeding on the lichens which grow on them. Being itself of a grey colour with black spots, it closely resembles in tint the lichen-covered rocks among which it lives. Elsewhere it is found only in north-west Spain and Portugal, and it is one of the most remarkable members of the Hiberno-Lusitanian fauna whose origin is discussed in the account of the Irish fauna in the " Ireland " volume of this series. Next in interest come two Limnæas, *L. involuta* and *L. prætenuis*, extreme forms of the *pereger* group, both confined to Ireland ; the former known only from the Killarney-Glengariff area, the latter occurring also in the district around Belleek in the north-west of Ireland. A closely allied form occurs on Achill Island, West Mayo. Another rare species, *Pisidium hibernicum*, is found in this Killarney-Glengariff area. It occurs also in Galway and in Sweden. Muckross, near Killarney, is the only Irish station for *Vertigo minutissima*. It will thus be seen that the Killarney district is one of extraordinary interest for the conchologist. There are other interesting areas in Munster. In the Suir valley, *Paludina vivipara* has recently been turned up in numbers in a fossil condition in the foundations of the bridge at Waterford—a species not known as living in Ireland—

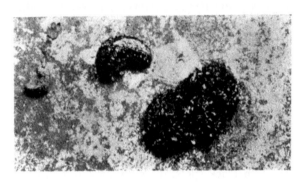

The Kerry Slug (*Geomalacus maculosus*)
beside the lichen on which it feeds

and *Helicigona lapicida*, hitherto unknown in Ireland, has recently been discovered living at Fermoy on the Blackwater. The Burren district in Clare is famous for the race of enormous *Helix nemoralis* that lives in the chinks of its limestone rocks. These resemble the German Pleistocene form *H. tonnensis*, Sandberger. Other interesting Munster species are : *Hyalinia lucida* (widespread, except in the west), *Zonitoides excavatus* (throughout the province, off the limestone), *Helicella barbara* (widespread, both on the coast and inland), *Hygromia granulata* (locally plentiful), *Acanthinula lamellata* (in every county), *Cæcilioides acicula* (local), *Pupa anglica* (in every county), *Vertigo Lilljeborgi* (Lough Allua, W. Cork, very rare), *V. pusilla* (very

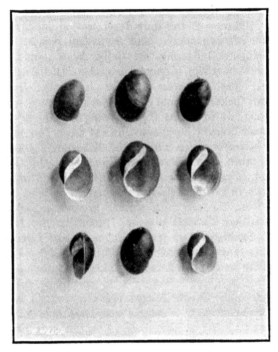

Limnæa prætenuis

local), *Succinea oblonga* (Kerry, Cork, Tipperary, Clare), *Paludestrina confusa* (estuaries of the Shannon, Suir and Barrow), *Acicula lineata* (widespread), *Margaritana margaritifera* (local).

The district from which many of the more interesting butterflies and moths come is Killarney, that favoured home of rare species, both animal and vegetable. Kerry, Cork and Waterford between them supply almost all the stations for the scarcer forms. Among the butterflies, Killarney is the only Irish station for *Argynnis latonia*, *Melitæa athalia*, and *Syrichthus malvæ*. Other rare Munster butterflies are *Colias hyale* (appeared in numbers in 1868), *Gonepteryx rhamni* (Killarney and Dinas), *Thecla betulæ* (locally frequent), *Hesperia thaumas* (near Cork), and *H. sylvanus* (Killarney). From the long list of moths the following may be selected: *Leucania Loreyi* (Queenstown, an extremely rare insect) ; *Sesia scoliæformis* (Kenmare and Killarney) ; the Lime Hawk-moth, *Smerinthes tiliæ* (Killarney) ; the Galway Burnet, *Zygæna pilosellæ*, var. *nubigena* (limestone pastures of northern Clare, elsewhere in Ireland known only from the adjoining similar ground in Galway) ; the southern *Lithosia caniola* (Tramore) ; the Lobster Moth, *Stauropus fagi* (two specimens near Kenmare) ; the rare *Notodonta bicoloria* (Killarney and Kenmare) ; *Leucania Loreyi* (two examples taken in Sussex in 1862 and one at Queenstown in 1910 constitute the only records in the British Isles) ; the southern *L. vitellina* (Courtmacsherry) ; *Nonagria sparganii* (not rare between Old Head of Kinsale and Glandore : in England only in Kent) ; *Aporophyla australis* (sandhills in Waterford) ; the southern *Laphygma exigua* (Timoleague, Co. Cork) ; *Agrotis rapæ* (sandhills at Rossbeigh, Kerry) ; *Tæniocampa populeti* (Killarney) ; the rare melanic var. *Barrettii* of *Dianthœcia luteago* (coasts of Waterford and Cork) ; *Cucullea absinthii* (Timoleague, Co. Cork) ; *Helisthis peltigera* (Castlehaven and Crookhaven, Co.

Cork) ; *H. armigera* (Glengariff) ; *Tholomiges turfosalis* (Killarney, only Irish station) ; the geometer *Pericallia syringaria* (Cappagh, Co. Waterford) ; and the rare plume-moth *Platyptilia tesseradactyla* (Clare and Galway).

In the south-west, around Killarney and Glengariff, a number of interesting beetles are recorded, including the alpine *Leistus montanus* (on the mountains), the rare *Pelophilus borealis* (Killarney lake-shores), *Harpalus meloncholicus* (Glengariff, only Irish station), *Lebia crux-minor* and the long-horn *Anoplodera sexguttala* (both at Muckross, ditto), *Anisosticta xix-punctata* (Kenmare, ditto), *Elater præustus* (Glencar, ditto), the alpine *Pryopterus affinis* and *Aromia moschata* (Killarney and Kenmare), *Strangalia aurulenta* and the northern *Donacia obscura* (both Glengariff). Other beetles which in Ireland are known from Munster alone are *Carabus cancellatus* (Rosscarbery, only certain record for the British Isles), *Elaphrus uliginosus* (Gap of Dunloe and Glengariff), *Pterostichus aterrimus* (near Cork), and *Chrysomela sanguinolenta* (Rosscarbery). On the sea-shore of Cork and Kerry *Amara convexiuscula* and *Aepus Robinii* have been taken. On lake-shores and river-banks occur *Panagæus crux-major* (Finlough, Co. Clare), *Chlænius holosericeus* (Cork and Kerry), *Bidessus minutissimus* (rivers at Kenmare and Cork), and *Silpha dispar* (Lough Derg). The mountain beetles include *Carabus glabratus* and *C. clathratus* (both in several counties), and the beautiful *Chrysomela cerealis* (Knockmealdown), which is unknown elsewhere in Ireland, has been taken in Great Britain only on Snowdon. In spite of the remarkably mild climate of the south of Ireland, distinctively northern species are rather characteristic; such, for instance, as *Blethisa multipunctata* (marshes, frequent), *Pselaphus dresdensis* (Killarney), the Cockchafer *Melolontha hippocastani* (Cork and Kerry), *Lema septentrionalis* (Waterford and Cork), and *Otiorrhynchus blandus* (frequent). Against these there are very few distinctively southern forms. The following beetles may also be mentioned : *Claviger testaceus* (Waterford), *Silpha quadripunctata* (Clare and Waterford), *S. subrotundata* (common, as elsewhere in Ireland), the conspicuous *Timarcha tenebricosa* (Waterford and Tipperary), and the Holly-boring Weevil, *Rhopalomesites Tardyi*, so frequent in Ireland and so rare elsewhere, which is on record in this district from Cork and Kerry.

The Mitchelstown cave in Co. Tipperary, a cavern a mile and a quarter in length, is inhabited by *Porrhomma myops*, an interesting spider with degenerate eyes, elsewhere known only from the cave of Espezel, Dept. of Aude, in southern France. Another very rare Munster spider is *Tegenaria hibernica*, taken at Cork and Skibbereen, and found also in Dublin (abundant), Wicklow and S.E. Galway. This species is unknown outside Ireland, and has its nearest relatives in the Pyrenees. It is an interesting member of the old Hiberno-Lusitanian fauna which is described and discussed at some length in the *Ireland* volume of the present series. The following spiders have not so far been obtained in Ireland beyond the confines of Munster : *Prothesima longipes* and *Euophrys erraticus* (both Clare) ; *Xysticus lanio*, *Epeira adianta*, and *Hyctra Nivoyi* (all in Waterford) ; *Xysticus pini*, *Euryopis flavomaculata*, *Tmeticus rivalis*, *Hilaira montigena*,

Tetragnatha pinicola and *Mangora acalypha* (all from Kerry) ; *Teutana grossa* and *Hyptiotes paradoxus* (both Cork), and *Pholcus phalangoides* (Waterford, Limerick, Cork and Kerry). The following species are also worthy of mention :—*Micariosoma festivum* (Cork and Clare, also in Leinster) ; *Tegenaria atrica* (Cork and Limerick, also Dublin) ; *Stylocteton uncinus* (Kerry ; also in Ulster ; unknown outside the British Isles) ; *Pardosa purbeckensis* (Kerry ; also in Connaught ; like the last, unknown outside the British area). The following notable species occur in several Munster counties, and are widely spread in Ireland : *Cyclosa conica, Pisaura mirabilis, Dolomedes fimbriatus, Misumena vatia*, and *Angelena labyrinthica*.

Space does not permit of any account of the other groups of Arthropods or of lower forms, but brief reference may be made to a few miscellaneous species which are of special interest. Among the dragonflies, *Libellula fulva*, rare in Great Britain, has its only Irish station at Dingle, and *Somatochlora arctica*, an insect of arctic and alpine range, in Great Britain confined to a few Scottish mountains, occurs in Ireland only in Kerry. The only scorpion-fly found in Ireland is *Panorpa germanica*, taken at Blarney and Youghal. Among the Hemiptera, *Æpophilus Bonnairei* is an interesting member of the Lusitanian fauna already alluded to, being confined in its range to south (Dungarvan) and west Ireland, S.W. England, France and Spain, its habitat being between tide-marks. The large Grasshopper *Mecostethus grossus* occurs in Kerry — an insect with a puzzling range, but mainly northern. The fresh-water shrimp *Mysis relicta* has been taken in the Shannon at Portumna ; it is unknown in Great

Britain, ranging across Northern Europe and America. *Eisenia veneta* is an interesting earthworm, occurring, in the variety *zebra*, at Limerick. The species has a wide but discontinuous Mediterranean range, the Limerick form being known elsewhere only from Transcaucasia. The fresh-water sponge *Heteromeyenia Ryderi*, which is confined to North America and Ireland, is abundant in the district.

ANTIQUITIES

MUNSTER contains numerous antiquities both prehistoric and historic. Many of the former are to be seen in Co. Kerry, while the most striking group of ecclesiastical buildings in Ireland is situated on the rock of Cashel, Co. Tipperary. The largest county in Ireland, Cork, which forms part of the province, contains an unusually large number of prehistoric and later antiquities.

There is no native flint in the district, and, though it is probable that the neolithic population imported it from the north of Ireland, flint implements have rarely been found in this part of the country: a number of polished axes have been discovered, and, as dolmens, stone circles, and other megalithic remains abound, we may conjecture that the neolithic population was a large one and was organised into tribes; the erection of great stone monuments pointing to a considerable amount of social organisation and to an advanced form of religious belief. As the province contains some of the most fertile land in Ireland, it is natural that it should have been occupied and prosperous from early times. Numerous antiquities of Bronze-Age date have been found in the different counties, while the discovery of the so-called " Clare find " of gold ornaments indicates wealth in this precious metal. The great number of forts of all types scattered through the province show that it was well populated in prehistoric and later times; two of its principal cities, Waterford and Limerick, were founded by the Norsemen.

Among the finds of prehistoric objects the most remarkable is the " Great Clare find." It was discovered when a cutting was made for the Limerick and Ennis Railway in 1854, by a gang of workmen who were digging a piece of ground lying a little to the south of the railway bridge in Moghaun north, on the west of Moghaun fort, opposite the lake. The workmen undermined a stone cist, and the fall of one of the stones disclosed a mass of gold ornaments of various types —gorgets, necklets, bracelets, and some ingots. The value of the find has been stated to be about £6000 ; if it had been preserved entire it would have been the largest find of associated gold objects of Bronze Age date that has yet been discovered in Western Europe. Unfortunately most of the ornaments were sold to jewellers and melted down ; only a small number were preserved, some of which are now to be seen in the National Museum, Dublin.

Another interesting find was made at Mountrivers, Rylane, Coachford, Co. Cork, in May 1907, by two men when making a fence ; it included two gold fibulæ, a penannular copper ring, two bronze celts, and eleven amber beads. The find may be placed in the late Bronze Age, and is of importance as indicating trade relations between Scandinavia and Ireland at this early date.

There is little doubt that the amber was derived from the north. Irish gold ornaments have been found in Scandinavia and were probably bartered for amber, which was much prized in prehistoric times.

It is impossible in the space at our disposal to give more than a slight sketch of the principal archæological and architectural monuments of Munster ; it will therefore be understood that the following account is only intended to convey a general impression of some of the more important antiquities of the province.

An archæologist of repute, who has given some attention to the subject, considers it probable that there are more stone circles in Munster alone than in the whole of England.

Co. Clare is rich in megalithic remains of various kinds. The majority of the dolmens stretch in a broad band from the Burren in a south-easterly direction to Slieve Bernagh ; the monuments lie inland rather than on the coast. They are most abundant in the Burren, in the eastern portion of the county. The types vary, but the one most frequently met with is in the form of a stone box composed of four or more slabs with a cover. Mr T. J. Westropp, who has described the megalithic monuments of Clare, computed the total number at 172, including 84 dolmens and large cists.[1]

The dolmens of Co. Tipperary have been studied in some detail.[2] They number twenty-five, seven of which are in a fair state of preservation. The principal group is in the hilly district surrounding the village of Kilcommon. It is situated about 10 miles

[1] *Proceedings of the Royal Irish Academy*, xxvi., sec. C, p. 458.
[2] Crawford, *Journal of the Royal Society of Antiquaries of Ireland*, xl., p. 38.

north of Dundrum station and twelve miles north-east
of Oola station. Here can be seen the remains of eleven
dolmens in a more or less ruined condition, and the sites
of four others, spread over a tract of land about seven
miles from east to west and four miles from north to
south. In the same district are the remains of four or
more stone circles. The best preserved dolmen in the
county is situated at Baurnadomeeny East. It lies about
a quarter of a mile north of the village of Rear Cross,
in a valley to the east of the road, with its axis running
east and west; it measures 24 ft. in length and 10 ft. in
breadth. Its eastern end makes a rectangular chamber
10 ft. long, 4 ft. wide, and 4 ft. high: its roof is formed
of four large stones. The western chamber measures
nearly 7 ft. square and 3 ft. 6 in. high. The amount of
earth which still remains on the roof of the dolmen
points to it having been originally covered by a mound;
traces of a stone circle which formerly surrounded the
dolmen may also be observed.

Though the monuments differ much in size, all appear
to belong to one type—that is, "a long, low dolmen,
with sides parallel or slightly tapering towards the east,
and formed of two or three rows of upright stones placed
close together. The central, or perhaps more strictly the
eastern, part is a long, narrow chamber, roofed with
several large slabs, which are laid almost level or with a
slight slope towards the east. To the west of this is a
somewhat wider and shorter chamber, separated from the
former by one of the most massive stones in the whole
structure, and having its roof set at a somewhat higher
level."

Co. Cork contains numerous megalithic remains.
Borlase mentioned seventy-one dolmens, but many of

these were then in a state of dilapidation, and only represented by a single stone. A number of stone circles, standing stones, and carns are also to be seen in the county.

The dolmens of Co. Kerry number, according to Borlase, twenty-two. Two in the townland of Gortna-gulla may be mentioned, as they have been examined and planned in recent years. Both are wedge-shaped structures and belong to a type common in the South of Ireland.

Several stone circles of interest are also to be seen, among the most important being that of Liosavigeen, about three miles from Killarney. It consists of seven stones, which vary in height from 3 ft. to $3\frac{3}{4}$ ft., with an average breadth of 3 ft. They enclose a circle of about 17 ft. in diameter, and are themselves surrounded by a ring fort of earth with a diameter of 78 ft.

About 45 ft. south of the top of the rampart of the fort are two standing stones; they are 7 ft. apart, and the larger measures $7\frac{1}{2}$ ft. in height and 6 ft. 3 ins. in breadth; the smaller is nearly 7 ft. high and $4\frac{3}{4}$ ft. in breadth.

There are not many dolmens in Limerick, but the series of megalithic monuments at Loch Gur make the prehistoric remains of this county of interest. Loch Gur is a picturesquely situated lake about 3 miles north of Bruff. It appears to have been the centre of a Bronze-Age cemetery. The lake itself was probably sacred, and it is likely that the large number of antiquities that have been found in or near it were deposited as votive offerings. The remains include nine stone circles, a dolmen, an alignment or avenue of stones, and numerous pillar stones. At the east side

of the lake is a hill called Knockadoon ; at the northern
end of this is a mediæval castle called Bourchier's Castle,
and at the southern another, known as the Black Castle.
The district belonged to the Desmonds, and legends
connected with this family are still told by the country
people. The largest of the stone circles is some 150
feet in diameter and is flanked by an earthen bank.
Several of the stones which form it are of great size,
but it was repaired during the last century, and it is
unfortunately impossible to say whether all the stones
are now in their original position. The megalithic
monuments have recently been described and illustrated
by Sir B. C. A. Windle, F.R.S.[1]

Borlase assigns fifteen dolmens to Co. Waterford ;
of these Knockeen is remarkable. Situated about a
mile from Waterford city, it is of great size and
in good preservation. One of the covering slabs is
13 ft. long by 8 ft. wide, and weighs about ten tons ;
it is supported by six uprights. This dolmen belongs
to a type, fairly common in Waterford, which has
a main chamber and an outer chamber or portico.
About two miles further, on the main road, is another
dolmen in the townland of Gaulstown ; it is of the same
type as that at Knockeen, its cap-stone weighs about
six tons. Close to this is a smaller monument of the
cistvaen type, and about two miles further from these,
at Ballymotey, is a remarkable pillar stone. One other
large dolmen in the same district, situated in the townland of Ballynageeragh, a mile to the west of Dunhill,
may be mentioned. It is well preserved ; its cap-stone,
which measures 12 by 8 ft., is computed to weigh six
and three-quarter tons.

[1] *Proceedings of the Royal Irish Academy*, xxx., sec. C, p. 283.

Munster contains the largest number of forts of all the Irish provinces. The number has been estimated at 12,232 : there are 7593 forts in Connacht; 4651 in Leinster; and 4283 in Ulster. It is, however, certain that the actual number of forts in each of the provinces exceeds these totals.

Co. Kerry contains many forts of the Cashel type, the best-known example of these being Staigue Fort, situated in Kilcrohan parish, barony of Iveragh, Co. Kerry. It is composed of a circular wall 89 ft. in diameter, nearly 13 ft. thick at the base, and 7 ft. at the top. On the north and west sides the wall is 18 ft. high; the north side of the wall is still perfect, and the coping-stones are flags about 3 feet long; the construction of the wall is interesting, the stones being laid as headers and filled in with small stones. There is a square-headed doorway with sloping sides on the south; and there are two small chambers in the fort—one on the west and one on the north side. There are ten sets of stairs around the inside of the wall, leading to platforms and forming the most interesting feature of the fort.

The Kerry forts, containing stone huts, or *Clocháns*, are very numerous; they exist in hundreds, and in many cases are still intact. The remarkable early settlement in the south-west of the barony of Corka-guiney contains many such buildings. It consists of a group of structures which lie along the sea-coast between Ventry Harbour and Dunmore Head, about ten miles from Dingle. The settlement covers about four townlands and verges on three others; the remains cluster thickly round the lower parts of Mount Eagle and Beennacouma. It is not visible from the road, with the exceptions of the large forts of *Dún Beag* and

Kilvickadownig. This remarkable site contains 515 forts, numerous huts, pillar stones, and other remains. The most important building of the entire series is *Dún Beag* (the little fort), one of the most striking prehistoric antiquities of Ireland. It consists of a stone wall, which cuts off a promontory protected on the landward side by an elaborate system of earthen walls and trenches, the area enclosed being thus triangular in shape, defended on the seaward side with great precipices. The height of the fort is about 90-100 ft. above the level of the sea. The edge of the cliff was protected by a dry stone wall, of which about 18 ft. in length and 2 ft. 2 in. in thickness remains at the south point. One stone building or *Clochán* remains inside the fort; it is circular, with a diameter of about 37 ft.; it had a domed roof and a movable door. The great wall of the fort is 139½ ft. in length, and varies in width from 8 ft. to 11 ft. Its internal face batters by irregular stages marked off by terraces, which doubtless served the purpose of enabling the defenders to mount the walls and reconnoitre. The doorway is remarkable; it is nearly 7 ft. in height and the same in breadth, with a reveal for the reception of a movable door; to the west and east of it there are several chambers. It contained a *souterrain* which maintained a straight course for a distance of 45 ft. The defences on the landward side consist of an alternation of fosse and vallum. The fort has suffered from a restoration undertaken some years ago.

Kilvickadownig is another important fort belonging to this group; it contains within it three cells, and there is one outside. The wealth of antiquities in this early settlement is astonishing; there are 414 clochans,

2 promontory forts, 7 raths, 15 forts, 12 crosses, 18 standing and inscribed stones, including two oghams, 19 souterrains, and 29 other ancient buildings and enclosures, which make a total of over 500 ancient remains. It is not easy to estimate the earliest period at which this site was inhabited, but, judging from the inscribed stones, Christianity was introduced not long after the original settlement. From the scanty remains of personal antiquities recovered it would appear that the general standard of comfort was low. The site and its antiquities have been surveyed by Professor R. A. S. Macalister,[1] and any person proposing to visit the remains should first read over his monograph.

Caherconree, another promontory fort in the same county, is a triangular space on a spur situated a little below the summit of one of the Sliabh Mis mountains, commanding a magnificent view over the whole peninsula of Corkaguiney. It is situated at a height of some 2050 ft. above the sea-level. The fort is bounded on two sides by precipices, and on the mountain side by a stone wall 350 ft. long and about 15 ft. thick, now very ruinous, composed of the native rock (Old Red Sandstone). The facing stones are laid as headers ; there is a shallow fosse outside. The gates are defaced. There is no indication of any buildings independent of the wall inside the enclosure : a number of trial pits which were sunk in the fort in 1910 revealed nothing but a thick mass of loose stones underneath about 3 ft. to 4 ft. of soft turf bog. *Caherconree* (the fort of Curaoi) has the following legend, belonging to the Cuchulainn saga, connected with it :—Curaoi was King of West Munster about the first century A.D. Cuchulainn,

[1] *Transactions of the Royal Irish Academy*, xxxi., pp. 209-344.

the chief hero of Ulster, was in love with Curaoi's wife, Blanaid, who returned his passion. Taking an opportunity, when most of Curaoi's men were absent from the fort, Blanaid gave the signal to Cuchulainn by pouring milk into the stream that runs down the mountain, which was afterwards named the *Fionnghlaise* (white stream). Cuchulainn, on seeing the stream become white, stormed the fort, killed Curaoi, and carried off Blanaid.

A Munster earthwork that has claimed much attention is the mote of Knockgraffon, near Clonmel, Co. Tipperary. It is one of the finest motes in Ireland, measuring some 55 ft. in height, with a diameter of about 60 ft. on the top; it is surrounded by a fosse, and has a hatchet-shaped bailey about 70 paces long by 57 wide attached to it at the western side. The bailey has a slight rampart round the edge, and beyond this a wide fosse and high vallum, the fosse of the bailey joining that of the mote. Mr G. H. Orpen, who considers Knockgraffon to be a Norman mote, has identified it with the castle of Knockgraffon which the *Annals of the Four Masters* record as having been built by the English of Leinster in 1192, in the course of their expedition against Domhnall Ó Briain king of North Munster. Other archæologists have ascribed an earlier date to this mote, and considered it to be the fort of Fiachaidh Muilleathan, who was king of Munster in the third century A.D. It is probable that Knockgraffon originally was a Celtic tumulus which was later used by the Normans as a site for a mote castle.

Another good example of a mote is situated at Lismore, Co. Waterford. It is a lofty conical mound with a flat top, divided by a fosse from a crescent-shaped bailey.

m H

King John erected a castellum at Lismore in 1185 A.D.; probably the mote and bailey represent this.

No less than five-sixths of the known Irish Ogham inscriptions have been found in Munster. Kerry contains 120 inscriptions, or one-third of the total. More than 60 of these are in the barony of Corkaguiney. There are some 80 inscriptions in Co. Cork and about 40 in Co. Waterford.

Lake Dwellings, or Crannogs, are not so numerous in Munster as in the other provinces, but several are important and have been found to contain antiquities valuable for the study of archæology.

The Crannog of Lough Gur, Co. Limerick, has yielded a number of objects of various descriptions at different times; unfortunately it has not been scientifically excavated, it is therefore difficult to form any opinion as to when it was first inhabited. The antiquities, stated to have been recovered on various occasions from this site, include a remarkable bronze spear-head with the socket inlaid with gold; part of a stone mould for casting socketed, and looped, spear-heads; an iron sword of late date; numerous stone celts, and various objects of bronze.

The decorated High Crosses to be seen in this province number some twenty-one; they are distributed among the counties of Clare, Kerry, and Tipperary; none are recorded from the counties of Cork or Waterford.

One of the most interesting is the cross of Dysert O'Dea, near Corofin, Co. Clare. It stands about 150 yards east of the church of Dysert Tola, on a small mound, and springs from a quadrangular base, upon which is a large block which supports the shaft, head, and cap. The base of the cross is carved with inscriptions stating that it was newly repaired by Michael O'Dea in 1683, and re-erected by Francis Hutcheson Synge in 1871. The north side of the base is carved with a figure holding a crosier of the usual Irish form, while two other figures hold a large tau-shaped crosier. On the east face of the shaft is the effigy of St Tola wearing a mitre and holding a crosier; on the head of the cross is a representation of the Crucifixion. The north and south sides of the shaft, and the west face, are decorated with various zoo-morphic, interlaced, and linear, patterns.

Other High Crosses of interest are those at Ahenny, Co. Tipperary. They are situated in a graveyard formerly called Kilclispeen, about 4 miles north of Carrick-on-Suir. Neither of the crosses contain panels with figure sculpture representing Biblical or other scenes; they are covered with every kind of spiral, interlaced, and fret patterns. The bases of both crosses are remarkable. On the west face of the north cross are carved seven figures, six of them holding crosiers: on the east is a man standing under a palm tree, with a number of animals in various attitudes in front of him. On the north side is a carving of a chariot and two mounted figures: on the south side is a representation of a procession; it is headed by men holding a ringed cross and a crosier, then comes a horse carrying on its back the headless body of a man upon which are perched two large birds who peck the flesh; the procession ends with a man carrying a child on his back. The base of the south cross is in a worn state, and the carvings of the panels are much defaced: they represent hunting scenes.

Another cross that deserves mention is the curious

tau-shaped example at Kilnaboy, about three and a half miles north-west of Corofin, Co. Clare. This T-shaped cross, measuring 2½ ft. in height, is fixed into a boulder. Two remarkable faces are carved on its upper surface, one on each side of the head.

The islands off the coast of Kerry contain some interesting early ecclesiastical remains.

The monastery on Skellig Rock is difficult of approach, except in good weather. It is one of the most curious primitive ecclesiastical settlements in Western Europe. The monastery was dedicated to St Michael : it is built on a rock which rises perpendicularly out of the sea to a great height, standing out in the Atlantic twelve miles from the nearest land. The remains consist of six small *clocháns* or stone huts built of dry stones with corbelled roofs ; the oratory of St Michael, which is the only structure built with mortar in the monastery ; three other dry stone oratories ; two large and a number of small crosses ; a cashel or stone fort encloses the buildings and surrounds the edge of the precipice.

The island was formerly a resort for pilgrims who used to ascend the " Way of the Cross," various points of the cliffs being named after the different stations of the Cross. There still remain six hundred steps cut out in the cliff, which rises to 720 ft. above the sea. The lower portion of the ascent is now broken away.

The Blasket Islands are twelve in number. The largest, Inismore, has the ruins of an ancient church and a graveyard. There are the ruins of a church and a nearly perfect *clochán*, with the foundations of several others, on Inisvickillane, the most southerly of the islands.

Some of the Armada ships were wrecked off the Blaskets, and about seventy years ago the islanders fished up a small brass cannon ornamented with a shield of arms bearing an uprooted tree.

ARCHITECTURE

Monastic Foundations

Previous to the dissolution of the monasteries there were close on one hundred religious foundations in the province of Munster. Many of these were communities of importance; their ruins add much to the picturesqueness and interest of the province. In spite of the Reformation Ireland remained substantially a Roman Catholic country, and in many cases small bodies of monks faced the danger of persecution and returned in the seventeenth century to Ireland, leading a furtive existence amid the ruins of their former homes.

One of the most interesting of the monastic remains in Munster are the ruins of Holy Cross Abbey, Co. Tipperary. This abbey was founded in 1169 A.D. by Domhnall Ó Briain king of Limerick, for monks of the Cistercian order; its possessions were confirmed to it by King John. A portion of the true Cross which had been presented to Donnchadh Ó Briain by Pope Pascal II in 1110 was preserved in a jewelled shrine of gold in the abbey, to which it gave its name : the monastery owed much of its wealth to offerings made by pilgrims at this shrine. The remains of the abbey are extensive ; the cruciform church consists of an aisled nave, choir, transepts with eastern chapels, and a square tower at the junction of the nave and choir. The eastern portion of the church has two storeys, the upper having probably served as a dwelling. The church was much altered and rebuilt in the thirteenth, fourteenth, and fifteenth centuries; few traces of the original Romanesque building can now be seen. The fine east window is reticulated,

Holy Cross Abbey, Co. Tipperary

while those of the transept-chapels are filled with flowing tracery of Flamboyant type. The eastern portion of the church has many ornamental details, there being two especially remarkable pieces of carving, one in the chancel and the other in the south transept. That in the chancel is known as the " Tomb of the Good Woman's Son," but was evidently the sedilia. It has three arches with foliage cusps and

tracery surmounted by a canopy ; above the arches are
shields carved with the royal arms of England, of
Butler, and of Desmond. It is probably of early fifteenth century date. Between the south transept chapels
is the remarkable structure which has been sometimes
considered to have been the sanctuary in which the relic
of the Holy Cross was preserved ; it is, however, more
probable that it was a " waking chamber," a receptacle
for a coffin. The roof of this monument is elaborately
groined : the supporting pillars have twisted shafts,
with bases, but no capitals ; the panelling below the shafts
is carved with foliage similar to that on the sedilia :
it is apparently of the same date. There are not many
remains of the conventual buildings ; the cloister, which
lay to the south, is now covered with grass ; the cellarium
still exists at the west end : above this was the dorter
of the lay brothers. The buildings on the south side
of the cloister have disappeared.

Another large and imposing monastic ruin to be seen
in the province is the Augustinian Priory of St Edmund,
at Athassel, Co. Tipperary. It was founded about
1200 A.D. by William de Burgo, and dedicated to St
Edmund, King and Martyr. It became an important
foundation, and its prior was summoned to parliament
as a peer. Both Walter and Richard de Burgo were
buried in the monastery. The priory owed much to the
de Burgo family, and there are several monuments in the
church which probably belong to members of this house.
At the dissolution it was granted to Thomas earl of
Ormonde. The buildings covered a large extent of
ground occupying about an acre, without the entrance
gateway and courtyard. The main buildings are
probably of thirteenth century date. The church is

cruciform with an aisled nave, transepts with eastern chapels, a choir and a central tower, with a flanking tower at the north-west angle of the nave. The cloister lay to the south of the church, and around it the conventual buildings were arranged. The original cloister arcade was probably of wood ; the remains of the cloister at present to be seen date from the fifteenth century.

The Dominican Friary at Kilmallock was founded in 1291 A.D. The remains of the church and conventual buildings are considerable. The church consists of a choir, and nave with a single aisle ; a tall, square tower rises from the junction of the choir and nave ; there is a single transept to the south, and a small sacristy to the north, of the choir. The conventual buildings lie to the north ; the day-room of the Friars and the kitchen are in good preservation. The window in the choir, which consists of five slender lancets, is of pleasing Early-English design. There are several tombs of interest in the choir, the best known being the broken slab which marks the grave of Edmond the last White Knight, a descendant of the reputed founder of the Priory. Edmond the White Knight betrayed his kinsman, the *Súgán* Earl of Desmond, in 1601, when the latter had taken refuge in the cave of Mitchelstown, Co. Cork. The White Knight received as a reward the sum of £1000 ; he died in 1608 ; his estates finally passed in the female line to Lord Kingston.

Ennis Friary, Co. Clare, is worthy of mention, not so much on account of its architectural interest as for the remarkable monuments that it contains.

The monastery was founded in the first half of the thirteenth century by Donnchadh Cairbrech Ó Briain,

King of Thomond, for Friars Minor. It was enlarged by Toirrdhealbhach Ó Briain at the end of the thirteenth century, and was further enlarged in the fourteenth and fifteenth centuries. The ruins of the church consist of a chancel and nave with a lofty tower at their junction.

Ennis Friary, Co. Clare

The most important of the monuments is the so-called Royal or MacMahon tomb, which is built against the north wall of the chancel near the east gable. It was at one time a mere heap of stones, but the sculptured slabs were rebuilt about 1843. The carved slabs have been described as being " probably the finest and most spirited series of late fifteenth-century carvings of the Passion in our Irish monasteries." The subjects include, the Betrayal of our Lord, the Flagellation, the Crucifixion, the Entombment, and Resurrection. The ancient canopy of this tomb fell down in recent times, and a modern one, imitated from that of the Inchiquin tomb, was erected in its place. The second canopied tomb stands against the south wall of the chancel and is probably of late fifteenth century date. It covers the graves of King Toirrdhealbach; Cu-Meadha Mac-Conmara; and some of the Lords Inchiquin. It is decorated with some gracefully carved floral designs.

The Franciscan Friary of Askeaton, Co. Limerick, is a ruin of large extent and considerable interest. It stands on the east bank of the River Deel. The buildings include a church and transept to the north, with a cloister, which is in good preservation, to the south.

Another Franciscan house that deserves mention is the monastery of Kilcrea, Co. Cork. Commonly called Kilcrea Abbey, it was founded in 1465 A.D. by Cormac MacCarthaigh, Lord of Muskerry, and dedicated to St Brigid. The church consists of a choir and nave with a south aisle, and a transept, with a lofty tower at the junction of the choir and nave. The cloister, surrounded by the conventual buildings, is to the north. The architecture is plain, and the lofty tower, about 80 ft. high, is the most striking feature of the ruin. The priory had a curious history; at the dissolution it was granted to Sir Cormac MacTaidhg, who did not disturb the Friars. In 1596 the convent was leased to Richard Harding, who also does not appear to have turned out the Friars. It was looted in 1599, but in 1604 the Friars returned. In 1614 it was again granted away by the Lord Deputy, one of the conditions being that the Friars should be driven out.

Trinitarian Friary, Adare, Co. Limerick

The ecclesiastical remains at Adare, Co. Limerick, are picturesque and interesting. Situated close to Adare Manor, the seat of the Earl of Dunraven, they consist of the ruins of three monasteries : one founded for Trinitarian Friars, another for Augustinian Hermits, and the third for Franciscan Friars Observant. The Trinitarian monastery was founded in 1230 A.D. ; the present remains consist of the church, and one wall of the buildings which composed the north side of the cloister, with a large tower at the western end, and a smaller one at the eastern end. The church has a nave, chancel and north transept, and a square central tower, with an embattled roof, at the junction of the nave and chancel. The north transept was lengthened and converted into a convent schoolroom in the last century. The church was repaired, enlarged, and the chancel rebuilt in 1852. Near it is an interesting low dovecot of circular form with a conical stone roof.

The Augustinian monastery was founded for Hermits of the order of St Augustine in 1315 by John earl of Kildare. The remains include the church, the cloisters, the refectory, and a long building extending to the north. The church consists of a chancel, a nave with a south aisle, and a square tower at the junction of the nave and chancel. This building was later converted into a Protestant church ; its architecture does not call for remark. Attached to the north-east angle of the building, on the north side of the cloisters, is a gateway with two shields over the arch, one bearing the arms of the Desmond FitzGeralds, the other those of the Leinster FitzGeralds. These shields probably commemorate the founders of this portion of the building. The ancient dovecot attached to the priory is still in existence.

The Franciscan Friary was founded in 1464 by Thomas earl of Kildare, and his wife Joanna. It was one of the most celebrated convents in the province of Munster, and, though of moderate size, is of interest owing to the completeness of its various buildings, being a good example of the Irish monastic architecture of the fifteenth century. The remains consist of a church with a nave, square tower, and chancel, a south transept

Franciscan Friary, Adare, Co. Limerick (south view)

with two eastern chapels, and a western aisle. The cloister is on the north side, and the conventual buildings can be well studied, several of them being in a good state of preservation. Among the most interesting features of the church are the remains of painted mural decoration which can still be observed.

Corcomroe Abbey, situated in the limestone hills of Co. Clare, was founded by Domhnall Ó Briain about

1182. The remains include a church and small cloister, with some domestic buildings to the east. The church is cruciform. The nave is plain, but the chancel and chapels contain interesting architectural details of the transitional period.

Cathedrals [1]

The cathedral churches of the province of Munster are in many cases interesting buildings ; among them is the ancient cathedral on the rock of Cashel, which includes Cormac's chapel, perhaps the most important Romanesque building in Ireland.

Taking the cathedrals in alphabetical order, the first is Aghadoe (*Achadh dá eó*, the field of the two yew trees), the bishopric of which has for many centuries been united with that of Ardfert. The remains of the ecclesiastical buildings include the base of a round tower, another circular tower, and a small ruined church known as the cathedral. The latter is a small building consisting of a nave and chancel ; there is a fine Romanesque doorway in the nave and two lancet windows in the chancel.

Ardfert (*Ard fearta*, the height of the grave) is a small village near Tralee in Co. Kerry ; the cathedral is a building of much interest ; though now roofless it is otherwise fairly complete. It was unroofed during the rebellion of 1641, but the transept was roofed and used as a parish church until 1871. The main body of the cathedral was probably built about the middle of the thirteenth century, being erected as a simple rectangle, but a large

[1] The writer has received assistance in writing notes on the Cathedrals from *The Cathedral Churches of Ireland*, 1894, by the late T. M. Fallow, F.S.A.

transept was added to the south side in later times, and it was probably at the same time that the main wall was embattled. The west doorway and its arcade is the most interesting portion of the building, being a fine specimen of Romanesque architecture. It is a

Corcomroe Abbey, Co. Clare

portion of an older Romanesque building, which formerly occupied the site of the present cathedral.

Ardmore (the great height), Co. Waterford, became the seat of a bishopric in the fifth century, but it was absorbed into the see of Lismore at the end of the twelfth century, and, though among the ruins there is a building called the cathedral, it can hardly be con-

sidered as a cathedral church. The ecclesiastical
ruins at Ardmore are of considerable interest. They
include a small stone oratory, the church known as the
cathedral, a round tower, St Declan's well, and close
to the latter the remains of a church known as *Teampull
Deisceirt* (Church of the South). Of these the oratory,
a small oblong building, is the oldest. It has been repaired and has a modern slated roof, put up in 1716 A.D.
by Dr Thomas Mills bishop of Waterford. A stone
engraved with an ogham inscription was built into the
gable. The building measures 13 ft. 4 in. by 8 ft. 9 in.,
with walls about 2½ ft. thick; the door is square-headed.

The cathedral consists of a nave and chancel; it has
a remarkable series of panels on the outer west face,
containing representations of various scriptural and
other scenes. The pointed east window of the chancel
has been built up; the chancel arch is a fine piece of
transitional architecture. An ogham inscribed stone
was found in the north wall of the chancel.

Only the western wall and more eastern part of the
south wall of *Teampull Deisceirt* remain, and the building
does not contain any architectural features of interest.

St Declan's well is close to the west end of the
church; it is covered by a small building supposed
to have been erected about 1798. Three curious representations of the Crucifixion are built into it. This well
was formerly a favourite resort, and twelve to fifteen
thousand pilgrims are stated to have visited it at St
Declan's pattern in 1841.

The round tower stands about 66 ft. from the cathedral
and is a very perfect specimen of these structures. It
measures 95 ft. 4 in. in height, and is decorated with
string-courses of sandstone.

Cashel took its name from the stone fort (*caiseal*) which was erected there in the fifth century by a King of Munster. The round tower is the oldest of the remaining group of buildings, probably dating from the tenth century ; the small, but beautiful, Romanesque church, known as Cormac's chapel, which was founded by Cormac MacCarthaigh king of Desmond and bishop of Cashel, in 1127 A.D., comes next in date, while the cathedral belongs to the end of the thirteenth century. The round tower is now incorporated in the cathedral at the north-east angle of the north transept, there being a doorway into it from the triforium. The tower is about 85 ft. in height, with a circumference of 51 ft. ; the walls are about 4 ft. in thickness. It has a round-headed doorway nearly 12 ft. above the ground.

Cormac's chapel is a beautiful specimen of Romanesque architecture ; it consists of a nave and chancel, with a square tower on each side in the position occupied by the transepts in later churches, making the plan of the chapel cruciform. The towers act as buttresses and support the thrust of the vaulting and of the heavy stone roof. The nave measures 29 ft. 8 in. by 17 ft. 8 in., and it is roofed by a barrel vault ; the chancel has a groined roof and measures 13 ft. 8 in. by 10 ft. 10 in. Both nave and chancel have crofts with a second stone roof above them. The south tower has a square embattled top, but this is a later addition. Originally it had a conical cap like the north tower. The chief interest of the chapel is its decoration, both inside and outside. The arcading is most elaborate, having panels which were painted with diaper work, while there were figure subjects on the walls and ceilings. The principal entrance is on the north, where the round-headed doorway consists

m I

of five orders with a high pediment over the arch. There are a varied and interesting series of carvings on the capitals, and over the doorway in the tympanum there is a curious figure of a centaur shooting a lion.

The cathedral is an aisleless cruciform building with a square tower at the junction of the nave and choir. Its internal length is 166 ft. 9 in. and width 132 ft. 8 in. Cormac's chapel was connected with the east side of the south transept; it was entered by a doorway opened in the west gable of the chapel in the transept. The nave of the cathedral is short compared to the choir, and it has been suggested that part of the length of the nave was cut off and is now occupied by the castellated structure at the west end. This latter structure was probably built about the end of the fourteenth century and used as a residence by the archbishop; the central tower of the cathedral was probably built about the same time. In 1495 Garrett earl of Kildare burnt the cathedral, and when asked by Henry VII his reason for doing this, replied that he had burnt the cathedral because he thought the archbishop (David Creagh) was inside it. At the southern part of the enclosure are buildings, probably erected in the fifteenth century, for the Vicars Choral. The Vicars Choral were constituted a corporation for the purpose of owning land: they had a curious seal, having for its device the pipes of the organ, the organist, and eight choristers. The cathedral was damaged by Cromwell's soldiers; but it was repaired in 1686, and restored in 1729: in 1748 Arthur Price, archbishop of Cashel, having unroofed and dismantled it, obtained an order from the Privy Council constituting the parish church of St John's, Cashel, the cathedral church of the diocese. Upon the disestablishment of the Irish Church the buildings on the rock of Cashel were vested in the Irish Board of Works to be preserved as a National Monument. The modern cathedral of Cashel is built in the Georgian style; it is a parallelogram in plan and has a tower with a spire at the west end.

Cloyne (*Cluain*, a meadow) is a small town situated about 4 miles from Midleton, Co. Cork; a bishopric was founded here in the sixth century by St Colman. The See of Cloyne has undergone various changes, having been united to Cork from 1431 until 1638; it was united to Cork and Ross from 1660 to 1678, and was a separate bishopric from 1678 to 1835, after which it was again united to Cork, forming the diocese of Cork, Cloyne, and Ross. The ancient cathedral is still in use: it is a low building cruciform in plan, and mainly of thirteenth century date. It appears never to have had a tower, the bells having been hung in the round tower which stands about 50 yards to the north-west of the cathedral. The woodwork screen which divides the nave from the choir is Georgian in type, and is of some interest.

Cork (*Corcach*, a marsh): the See of Cork was founded by St Finn Barr in the early part of the seventh century. The ancient cathedral was demolished in 1735, and a small Georgian church built to replace it. No account of the earlier cathedral exists. The Georgian cathedral was replaced in 1865 by the present cathedral designed by Mr W. Burgess, R.A., and consecrated in 1870. It is an imposing cruciform church built in the French-Gothic style.

Emly (*Imleach*, a marshy place): the See of Emly was founded by St Ailbhe in the fifth century. The ancient cathedral church was destroyed in 1828 and a poor modern building erected in its stead.

Kilfenora (*Cill Fionnabhrach*, the church of Fionn-abhair) is about 18 miles from Ennis, Co. Clare. One of the smallest and poorest dioceses in Ireland, it has had no separate bishop since the seventeenth century. The cathedral is a small building consisting of a nave and choir with a bell turret at the west end of the nave ; there is a sacristy attached to the eastern walls of the choir. The nave is now used as the Protestant parish church ; the choir and sacristy are roofless. The choir, which is the most interesting portion of the building, has a fine east window of three lights, with round-headed arches.

Killaloe (*Cill Dhá-Lua*, the church of Dá Lua), Co. Clare, is situated about 17 miles from Limerick. The See was founded by St Lua in the seventh century. The cathedral, which is of thirteenth century date, is an aisleless, cruciform building, with a square, massive, central tower. An interesting Romanesque doorway is built into the western corner of the south wall of the nave ; it consists of an arch of four orders, with richly decorated carved shafts, capitals, and bases.

Limerick (*Luimneach*, a bare spot of land) : the See of Limerick is generally considered to have been founded as early as the fifth century. The interesting cathedral was probably erected during the twelfth and the thirteenth centuries. The earliest ground plan appears to have been in the form of a Latin Cross, but side aisles were added to the nave in the fourteenth and fifteenth century, which have obscured the original outline of the plan. An embattled square tower with four turrets stands at the west end. Limerick is unique amongst the Irish cathedrals in possessing carved wood-work of the fifteenth century ; its stalls, with carved misereres, ornamented with various grotesque devices, resemble those which have been preserved in many English cathedrals.

Lismore (*Lios mór*, the big fort), in Co. Waterford : the See of Lismore, founded by St Carthach in the seventh century, became one of the great schools of Ireland, and many notable names are connected with it, such as Cormac MacCarthaigh, and Malachias of Armagh. Lismore became " a famous and holy city, into the half of which (there being an asylum) no woman dare enter. It is filled with cells and holy monasteries, and a number of holy men are always in it. The religious flow to it from every part of Ireland, England, and Britain, anxious to remove thence to Christ." Most of the present cathedral dates from the seventeenth century, when it was rebuilt after it had almost been reduced to ruin by Edmond Fitzgibbon the White Knight. Some portions, such as the chancel arch and a few windows in the south transept, probably belong to the twelfth century. In plan the cathedral is a cruciform, aisleless church with a tower, crowned by a graceful spire at the west end. It contains an interesting sixteenth century altar tomb erected to the memory of John Magrath and his wife ; five early grave slabs inscribed in Irish are built into the west wall of the nave.

The bishopric of Ross (*Ros*, a wood), some 10 miles from Skibbereen, Co. Cork, is supposed to have been founded about the sixth century ; it became a famous seat of learning. The See has been united with Cork since 1583, the style of the diocese being that of Cork, Cloyne, and Ross. The cathedral was almost entirely rebuilt during the seventeenth century; it contains no architectural features of importance.

The ancient cathedral of Waterford was founded by the Norsemen about 1050 A.D. From extant plans and illustrations it appears to have been a building of much interest. By an act of vandalism it was completely pulled down in the latter part of the eighteenth century, when a new cathedral in the Georgian style was erected in its place.

Churches

The Oratory of Gallerus, situated Corkaguiney, Co. Kerry, is the most complete specimen of this type of building now to be seen in Ireland. It measures 23 ft. by 16 ft. externally; it is 16 ft. in height. It is built of dry stones; the doorway has inclined jambs. Near it is a stone pillar, ornamented with a cross in a circle, and incised with the name of Colum.

At Kilmalkedar, at the foot of Mount Brandon, is an interesting church of probably twelfth century date. It is surrounded by the ruins of a small early monastic settlement.

Another interesting church of early type is that of St Farannan at Donaghmore, between Clonmel and Fethard, Co. Tipperary. It is a small Romanesque building of good proportions, decorated with carving and cut-stone. The carvings on the west doorway are especially fine. The church consists of an aisleless nave, and a small chancel; it is built of uncoursed rubble containing large irregular stones with small ones between them. There is a rubble vault over the chancel; above this is a room with a small east window, entered by a doorway over the chancel.

The Church of St Peter and St Paul at Kilmallock, Co. Limerick, is interesting. It lies within the walls of the town and its chancel is used as the parish church. As well as an aisled nave, and chancel, there is a south transept, and attached to the north-east corner of the nave is a round tower about 50 ft. in height. The east window of the chancel has five lights. In the north aisle of the nave some interesting tombs are to be seen. The walls of the church were protected with battlements.

Castles

Cahir Castle, Co. Tipperary, is a picturesque example of Tudor building : as it now stands, it presents architecture of the fifteenth and sixteenth centuries, with the restorations carried out in 1840 by the Earl of Glengall. The castle, which occupies a large space, is irregular in outline : it consists of a square keep with extensive outworks, which form an inner and outer vallum. It became the property of the Butlers lords of Cahir, and still remains in the hands of their descendants in the female line. In 1599 it was described as the only famous castle of Ireland which was thought impregnable, a bulwark for Munster, and a safe retreat for all the agents of Spain and Rome. It was besieged by the Earl of Essex in 1599, by Lord Inchiquin in 1647, and a few years later by Cromwell.

The so-called " Desmond " Castle at Adare, Co. Limerick, was probably erected on the site of a Norman mote. The present ruins include a portion of the keep, the hall, out-rooms, and gate-tower. The buildings show so few architectural features that it is difficult to determine the dates of the various portions, but the keep may have been built in the thirteenth century. The modern mansion of the Earl of Dunraven is an imposing structure in the Tudor style; it was built in 1850 of limestone obtained from the district.

Carrick Castle, built in the fifteenth century by Edmond Butler, who died in 1464, is an interesting

The Keep, Desmond Castle, Adare, Co. Limerick

specimen of a Tudor manor-house. It is a large quadrilateral pile enclosing a central court. The ancient front is built in a castellated style ; it faces the Waterford mountains to the south, commanding a view of the vale between Clonmel and Waterford. The Elizabethan front is considered to have been built by Thomas earl of Ormonde and Carrick, who died in 1614. The castle is especially interesting on account of its north gallery, which is wainscotted with oak, and has stucco panels decorated with finely executed heraldic devices. The Marquis of Ormonde is the present owner of the castle.

Limerick Castle is stated to have been built by King

Thomond Bridge and King John's Castle, Limerick

John. At each of the north angles is a round tower, and one remains at the south-west. The gateway is in the centre of the north curtain wall. A view of the castle *circa* 1611 shows it to have been roughly oblong in plan, with the gateway and two angle towers on the northern end, while at the southern end there was a tower at the south-west angle and a bulwark for holding cannon on the south corner. A large store-house was attached to the western curtain wall. The castle was besieged by the Confederate Catholics in 1641, when, after a severe siege, the English garrison surrendered on terms.

Waterford Castle, generally known as Reginald's tower, is stated to be of Danish origin. It is circular in plan and some 80 ft. high. A tablet placed over the main entrance records that the tower was built in 1003 by Reginald the Dane, that it was afterwards held as a fortress by Strongbow, that it was later used as a mint, and finally turned into a police barracks.

The castle of Kiltinane, about 7 miles north of Clonmel, Co. Tipperary, on the River Glashauney, is a strong building standing on a rock over the river, into which there is a drop of 100 ft. on the eastern side. It consists of a quadrangular courtyard with three fortified towers, two of which form the modern house. The towers have walls of great thickness, and vaulted stone ceilings. The castle well has a passage leading to it down eighty-seven steps. This castle was one of the six granted by King John to Philip of Worcester. It afterwards passed into the possession of the Lords Dunboyne, and was held by them at the time of its capture by Cromwell in 1649. Later it became the property of Richard Staper, who in 1669 sold it to Peter Cooke, by whose descendants it is still occupied.

About 2 miles east of Clonmel is a mansion built in the Tudor style, with quadrangular windows divided by stone mullions. It was probably erected by Alexander Power in the reign of James I. It is known as Tickencor House.

In the same neighbourhood are the remains of the castle of Derrinlaur. The name *Doire an láir* signifies the

Middle-oak-wood, the neighbouring hills having been for many centuries covered with woods. The castle was probably one of the strongholds of the Butlers.

The remains of the ancient walls and the castellated houses at Kilmallock, Co. Limerick, are also worthy of mention.

ADMINISTRATION

MUNSTER, the largest province in Ireland, has a population of 1,035,495, and contains three of the six County Boroughs, viz., Cork, Waterford, and Limerick. These three County Boroughs have each a Mayor (Cork, a Lord Mayor) and Municipal Council, with their several committees. The county areas are under the control of the County Councils, which, with the other County Councils, were established by the Local Government (Ireland) Act of 1898. The Council, the members of which hold office for three years, is elected by the county electoral divisions, and performs numerous important duties, such as maintaining the main roads of the county, providing and managing lunatic asylums, etc. It has power to make bye-laws and to oppose Bills in Parliament and to prosecute or defend legal proceedings necessary for the promotion or protection of the interests of the county. The County Borough Councils are "administrative counties" and have similar powers to the County Councils. Urban sanitary authorities are called Urban District Councils, and rural sanitary districts have Rural District Councils. These Councils have wide powers and responsibilities in regard to public health and other matters concerning the public good.

Particulars as to the County Borough and County areas
are set out in the subjoined table:

(1)	Population (Census of 1911). (2)	Area on which the Valuation has been determined. (3)	Valuation on 1st March 1914. (4)	Number of Members of Parliament (see Note). (5)
		Acres	£	
County Boroughs				
Cork . . .	76,673	2,685	189,470	2
Limerick . .	38,518	2,386	75,819	1
Waterford . .	27,464	1,237	50,142	1
Maritime Counties				
Clare—				
Rural Districts	94,094	795,355	313,701 }	2
Urban Districts	9,138	1,800	12,987 }	
Cork—				
Rural Districts	274,358	1,840,196	1,034,215 }	7
Urban Districts	41,703	9,281	89,477 }	
Kerry—				
Rural Districts	140,186	1,165,094	283,604 }	4
Urban Districts	19,505	4,415	31,533 }	
Waterford—				
Rural Districts	51,525	451,323	260,028 }	2
Urban Districts	4,977	1,360	8,778 }	
Inland Counties				
Limerick—				
Rural Districts	104,551	667,519	476,905	2
Tipperary (N.R.)—				
Rural Districts	51,765	488,514	257,408 }	
Urban Districts	11,116	4,448	21,144 }	4
Tipperary (S.R.)—				
Rural Districts	64,650	553,023	370,336 }	
Urban Districts	24,902	4,669	42,738 }	

Note.—The boundaries of Parliamentary Divisions are not
coterminous with local administrative areas.

EDUCATION

The province is well supplied with educational agencies, from those of university type to elementary schools working under the Board of National Education. The University College (formerly Queen's College) of Cork is one of the constituent colleges of the National

University College, Cork

University, and has made a notable advance in recent years. Situated in an elevated and picturesque position in the western suburb of the city, it possesses charming buildings which were erected in 1849 on the site of the old Gill Abbey, from designs by Sir William Deane. There is a spacious examination hall, a library and museum. More recently the beautiful Honan Memorial Chapel has been added. The number of students, the majority of whom are Roman Catholics, has increased steadily during the last fifteen years. New engineering laboratories have been equipped, and the College is virtually a university for the southern province, though it does not enjoy this status, but is a constituent college of the National University of Ireland.

The provision for scientific and technical education is no less complete, and has developed greatly since the establishment of the Department of Agriculture and Technical Instruction in 1899. Under the direction of this Department of State the Technical Instruction Committees of the counties of the province have adopted schemes of technical instruction which not only provide specialised instruction in the smaller towns, but also by the agency of numerous well-trained itinerant instructors carry instruction in manual work in wood, farriery, domestic economy, art, home industries, etc., to the remotest districts. In some local centres classes in domestic economy are conducted by nuns who have been trained in courses specially organised for the purpose. The value of this teaching has been very marked, and it was certainly very much needed. No less marked has been the educational work of the Agricultural Committees of the County Councils, who, under their schemes, have carried instruction in agriculture, horticulture, dairying, poultry-rearing and such-like subjects to all parts of these southern counties. Indeed, it is naturally in the rural areas that the activities of the Committees of Agriculture have their full scope, while in the urban centres technical education other than agricultural finds its opportunity. In the city of Cork, for example, there is the fine Crawford Municipal Technical Institute. The Crawford Municipal School of Science and Art occupied the site of the old Custom-house. A fine building was opened in 1885, having been restored and enlarged at a cost of about £20,000 by the late Mr W. H. Crawford. It provided accommodation for classes in Science and for a School of Art, and had besides picture and statuary galleries and a public library. With the great forward movement in technical education which began with the present century this building was found

Crawford Municipal Technical Institute, Cork

to be inadequate to the needs of technical education, and during the last few years a handsome building has been erected and equipped in Sharman Crawford Street, with splendid engineering, chemical and physical laboratories, as well as class-rooms for various technological subjects and for domestic training. The School of Art, which, in addition to providing a general art training, has for many years done valuable work in training designers and workers for the lace industry, is carried on in the older building. The growing demand for commercial training led the City Technical Committee to secure and adapt premises in the Mall, where there now exists a largely attended and otherwise successful School of Commerce. The municipality also largely supports the School of Music. A scheme of co-ordination exists between University College and the Technical Institute, and engineering students of the former receive instruction in mechanical engineering at the Institute.

About a mile to the west of the city of Cork is the Munster Dairy Institute, a fine building which, surrounded by farm land, was reconstructed in 1876, and was known as the Munster Agricultural and Dairy School. It is now under the direct management of the Department, and serves to provide a thorough training in agricultural and domestic work for women students. The course includes dairy work, poultry rearing, gardening, and domestic economy, and the School serves as a training-ground for teachers of certain of these subjects.

Waterford has also a flourishing Technical Institute. For many years its operations were retarded by unsuitable premises, but a few years ago the Technical Committee, under the chairmanship of the late bishop, the most Reverend Dr Sheehan, who rendered conspicuous service to the cause of education, undertook the erection of a new school which is more adequate to the needs of this important town. In addition to the usual courses in Art, Science, and Technology, there is a Day Trades Preparatory School for boys preparing for an industrial career. Similarly in Limerick, after working under disadvantageous conditions for long years in the Athenæum and elsewhere, the Technical Committee prepared plans for, and a few years ago erected, a

Haulbowline

m K

handsome Technical Institute, which is providing higher instruction in Science, Art, and Technology.

Some of the smaller towns in Munster have also shown great progressiveness in the matter of technical education. Towns such as Queenstown (now Cobh), Tralee, and

Training College, Limerick

Clonmel have made noteworthy progress. Queenstown (Cobh), with the neighbouring dockyards at Haulbowline, has developed elementary instruction in engineering, though its buildings are still inadequate to its needs. Tralee has made amazing progress. A few years ago excellent work was carried on in old builders' workshops, to which entrance was gained through a yard bearing the uninviting notice, "All Funeral Requisites Promptly

Supplied," and only during the last year or two has a dignified and adequate building, providing for evening courses of instruction and a Day Trades Preparatory School, been erected for this busy and thriving western town. But in this case, as in that of all the others mentioned, considerable difficulty has been experienced. The Act of 1899, which provided a sum of £55,000 per annum for technical education, made no provision for buildings. Suitable buildings were almost non-existent. It has then become necessary in all the instances named to borrow money for the new buildings, the interest and repayment of which forms a heavy burden on the annual income of the committees, whose operations must of necessity be correspondingly restricted. Tipperary has a small school managed by a joint committee of the urban and rural districts.

There are two training colleges for national teachers in Munster—one for male teachers—the De La Salle Training College at Waterford—and one for female teachers at the Laurel Hill Convent at Limerick. Both colleges are lodged in excellent buildings.

The space available here will not serve to enter into any details respecting the secondary schools in the province, but it may be noted that they are very generally worked under the rules of the Intermediate Education Board. They are denominational in character, and Catholic schools are commonly conducted by a religious order. Near Cashel there is the large and important Secondary School known as Rockwell College. Other schools are conducted by the orders of the Christian Brothers and Presentation Brothers. Standing high above the city of Cork, on Our Lady's Mount, is the Christian Brothers Schools. These schools are remarkable in many respects. They possess fine physical and chemical laboratories, workshops (with power) for manual work in wood and metal, an extensive school museum, and other features bearing evidence of the enthusiasm and unselfish devotion of the late Brother Burke, to whom is due in large measure the success of

Ursuline Convent, Waterford

the schools and the direction of the education, which is well designed to fit the pupils for a future of usefulness. The Christian Brothers College is a smaller institution dealing with senior pupils. A noteworthy Secondary School for girls is the Ursuline Convent at Waterford, which has a successful department for domestic teaching. There are excellent Protestant schools of secondary type both for boys and girls.

INDUSTRIES & MANUFACTURES

MUNSTER is a dairying and cattle-raising province, and its interests, speaking generally, are agricultural. Nevertheless it has a number of flourishing manufactures, and the history of many of these are full of instruction. Perhaps the oldest and most permanent of these is the textile industry—mainly the weaving of woollen goods. It is not generally known, however, that the growing of flax and the spinning of this into yarns by hand was general throughout the county of Cork two hundred years ago. In the middle of the eighteenth century linen yarns were exported from the county to England, and there is extant an interesting letter dated 18th April 1752 from a London firm addressed " To the Yarn Makers of the Citty and County of Cork or elsewhere," asking for yarn. Flax was grown in West Cork (Dunmanway, Clonakilty, etc.). In 1851 there were no less than 5991 acres under flax in Munster, while in 1915 there were only 259 acres, of which 257 acres were in the county of Cork. There are three scutching mills, two worked by water and one by steam. In 1662 the manufacture of linen cloth was started in Charleville. About 1750 the manufacture began to flourish in West Cork. In that year there was a spinning school at Youghal. In 1726 the manufacture of sailcloth was carried on extensively at Douglas, near Cork. It is noteworthy that the first mill for the spinning of flax by machinery in Ireland was started in the city of Cork about the year 1800. It contained 212 spindles for the spinning of coarse, dry-spun yarns suitable for the manufacture of canvas and sailcloth, which were produced in considerable quantity in the city and county. It was not until close on thirty years after that the first movement was made to establish the trade in Belfast. It has since almost died out in the south, but has been revived by the Cork Spinning and Weaving Company, Ltd., of Millfield, which now employs over 900 persons in the spinning and weaving of flax for home markets.

In 1810 a cotton mill was erected near Bandon.

But it is the woollen industry which is really *native*, and which, in spite of many vicissitudes and much repressive legislation, has survived, is flourishing to-day, and gives promise of great development. Ireland was famous for its woollen industry and trade as far back as the twelfth century—several centuries before the English industry. In the twelfth and thirteenth centuries Irish friezes and serges were known and esteemed in the English markets, and in the fourteenth century were famed in Naples and other parts of the Continent. The early instruments of manufacture were, of course, the distaff and spindle, the hand-combs and the hand-loom. The shearing of the sheep was done by men, but the spinning and weaving were carried out by the women, who clothed themselves and their families with excellent, if rough, native cloth. But the growing trade suffered serious reverses. In the reigns of Henry VIII. and Elizabeth the jealousy of English manufacturers led to a systematic boycott of the Irish trade, which suffered considerably, and Irish woollen-workers were driven from Ireland to the Continent. By the amended Navigation Act of 1663 Ireland was prohibited exportation to English colonies. The trade, however, was partially re-established, and during the administration of Ormonde a mill was started in Clonmel and carried on by five hundred Walloon families, to whom were given land and houses on long and easy leases. The industry developed in Cork and elsewhere, and in the latter part of the seventeenth century expanded into an important export trade. As a result English woollen manufacturers became alarmed at Irish competition and took steps to stop it. In 1698 both Houses of Parliament addressed William III. upon the growing manufacture of cloth in Ireland and sought to have it stopped. A Bill was forced through the Irish House of Commons by which duties on all exports of drapery were imposed, ranging from 10 per cent. to 25 per cent. *ad valorem*. In the same year the English House of Commons passed a Bill forbidding exportation from Ireland to England or elsewhere of her woollen manufactures. The results were lamentable and the next half century was a period of extreme poverty. The recovery of the industry has been slow, due probably to the fact that those who brought about its re-establishment prior to 1698 were not native Irish, but Protestant immigrants from England, France, and Holland, who left the country owing to the suppression of their industry. They carried their skill and accumulated experience with them, and so the industry continued to wane. The recovery of this much-tried industry is comparatively recent. In the woollen and worsted spinning and weaving there were nine factories in 1853, and forty-three in 1863. There are to-day about eighty-five woollen factories in Ireland. Among the oldest of these is Messrs Martin Mahony & Bros., Ltd., of Blarney, who were established in the middle of the eighteenth century, and whose first power-looms were established in 1863. They have now over one hundred looms at work and a large spinning plant. They employ nearly six hundred hands, and export their woollen and worsted goods to the Colonies and various European countries. Messrs O'Brien Bros., Ltd., of Douglas, near Cork, employ over four hundred hands in the manufacture of tweeds, while Morrogh Bros. & Co., of Douglas, also employ a

Twisting Machines in a Woollen Factory

large number of hands. There are several other smaller but growing industries, and it is believed that the recent establishment of an Irish Woollen Manufactures Association may have an important influence on the development of this truly native industry. The manufacture of hand-woven goods is still carried on largely on the western seaboard.

In the cities of Cork and Waterford there are large

bacon-curing industries. In Cork also is the large clothing factory of Messrs Lyons & Co., the important chemical works of Messrs Harrington, and the two large breweries of Messrs Beamish & Crawford and Messrs Murphy. Tanning, which was so important an Irish industry in the past, is also carried on.

There are in the province over one hundred and seventy corn mills, of which over eighty are in the county of Cork. It is interesting to note that forty-seven of these are driven by water power, while eleven others employ both water and steam.

Cork is an important centre of distribution of dairy and other agricultural produce, and the Cork Butter Exchange, situated on the north side of the city, is one of the largest in existence.

There are some shipbuilding and engineering works and the most important of these is the Royal Dockyard at Haulbowline, in Queenstown (Cobh) Harbour, which gives employment to about a thousand men. The harbour itself is one of the finest in the world, and in pre-war days was a calling-place for transatlantic liners. It provides anchorage with 20 ft. of water alongside the jetties, and vessels of over 24 ft. draught can discharge at the deep-water quays.

The shipping industry is of great importance, and Cork has over four miles of quays. The principal trade is in grain, timber, coal, live stock, provisions, and whisky. Its interests are watched over by the Cork Incorporated Chamber of Commerce and Shipping. Reference must also be made to the Cork Industrial Development Association, which grew out of the Cork International Exhibition of 1902, which served a valuable end in drawing attention to the potentialities of Irish industries.

In the year following the exhibition some of the citizens of Cork formed themselves into an Association, and a year or two later summoned the first All-Ireland Industrial Conference, which has been followed by several others, to the great encouragement of the industries of the country.

Limerick has a small harbour, the accommodation of which is increased by the provision of a floating dock, 810 ft. long, and a graving dock of 428 ft. in length. The trade is mainly imports of wheat, maize, coal, and timber. There is a small export trade. The city is noteworthy industrially on account of its large bacon-curing establishments. It is stated that the three large establishments of Messrs Shaw, Matheson, and Denny together slaughter some ten thousand pigs a week. One of the principal industries also is the condensed milk factory of Messrs Cleeve. Near by at Adare, the seat of the Earl of Dunraven, interesting experiments have been for some time in progress on the growing of tobacco, and excellent cigarettes are manufactured in the village from tobacco thus grown.

Scattered throughout the province are home industries, some of which have attained to some importance. Principal among these is the making of lace. Flat Point Lace was first introduced into Ireland by the Sisters of the Presentation Convent at Youghal as a means of assisting the sufferers from the famine in the years 1847-50. It was founded on Italian models, but has been so much modified and enriched that it may be considered an Irish lace, and the industry has been greatly developed subsequently, most beautiful specimens of work having been produced both here and in the convent of Kenmare. A similar impulse originated the industries carried on with such success in the industrial department of St Joseph's Convent School at Kinsale, where lace-making is supplemented by drawn-thread work, embroidery, machine knitting, etc.

In Limerick, too, home industries have been encouraged, and " Limerick lace " is widely known. The industry was introduced nearly ninety years ago by an Englishman named Walker, who brought over a group of teachers and started lace-making in a disused store at Mount Kennet, the site of the present docks at Limerick. The industry took firm root. The Irish girls proved apt pupils, and in course of time large numbers of women and girls were employed. It flourished exceedingly during the first decade of the reign of Queen Victoria, and as many as six hundred women and girls found employment. The industry declined after the death of the Prince Consort and the consequent period of Court mourning, to which the decline in the trade was attributed. Doubtless also the introduction of inexpensive machine-made lace— good in design and execution—made in the English midlands was a powerful cause. Some thirty years ago efforts were made by Mrs Vere O'Brien to revive the industry, and with some success. Classes were established in George Street and at the Good Shepherd Convent, while lace was also made by several local firms. It is much to be regretted that the outbreak of war struck yet another blow at a struggling industry which produces so beautiful and artistic a product and on which so much voluntary labour has been bestowed.

Hand-spinning and weaving is still carried on as a home industry in some parts of the province, but the disadvantages of this mode of production led to the workers being gathered together under one roof where this was possible, and the weaving industry of the Convent of Mercy, Skibbereen, established by the Bishop of Ross, claims to have been the first to establish weaving within the walls of an Irish convent in recent times. The example thus set was followed by Queenstown (Cobh), Kilkenny, Carrick-on-Suir, and Stradbally (Waterford). Later it was, with other industries such as machine hosiery-knitting, embroidery, vestment-making, etc., started by the nuns of the Convent of Mercy at Gort (Co. Galway), and developed with considerable enthusiasm.

It is not possible to enumerate the various efforts made to stimulate home industries, but the valuable work of Miss Spring Rice at Foynes calls for mention.

AGRICULTURE

Munster is essentially a dairying and cattle-raising province, and prior to the war tillage had continuously decreased, while the number of cattle had correspondingly increased. The county of Limerick is famous for its fine pasture-land. and dairy farming is carried on extensively in the rich " Golden Vale " which constitutes a large part of the county. Cork too, especially the eastern portions of the county, has a rich soil. In the year 1851 there were 732,294 acres under corn crops and 403,973 acres under green crops in Munster. In 1915 these areas had been reduced to 284,946 and 260,304 areas respectively. At the same time the acreage of hay, which was 372,072 in 1851, had more than doubled by 1915. The great decline was in the amount of wheat grown. There was a great decline in the area of potatoes, but a large increase in cabbage. In 1918 mainly through the operation of the Compulsory Tillage Regulations, the area under corn crops was brought up to 420,271 acres, while the area under green crops had been raised to 286,210 acres.

Creamery, Tipperary

There were in the province in 1918 as many as 1,702,194 cattle, 174,063 horses, and 709,963 sheep.

In the matter of forestry it may be said that Munster has over 94,000 acres under forest trees, of which nearly 25,000 acres are in County Cork and nearly 24,000 in County Tipperary. As many as 293 acres were planted in the year ending 31st May 1915 with 649,459 trees, mainly conifers. In the same period 904 acres were cleared and over half a million trees felled.

FISHERIES

The sea and inland fisheries are of considerable value. In the seventeenth century pilchard fishing was general in West Cork and Kerry, Flemish vessels loading cargoes, whilst pirates found it worth while to watch for these vessels at sea. Pilchards were on the coast in the early half of the nineteenth century, but about 1880 they suddenly abandoned it. Hake also was taken in quantity inshore, and are now fished in from 50 to 200 fathoms from the Kerry coast, the catches being landed at Milford or Fleetwood. Spaniards had fishing stations on the coast in the sixteenth century, and many islands and bays on the south-west coast are still called " Spanish." Mackerel is the main southern fishery, and there is a spring and autumn mackerel fishery almost exclusively off the coast of Munster. The capture during the spring fishery of 1915 was the smallest for many years. The bulk of the fish were landed at Baltimore (where there is a Fishery School), amounting to 23,512 cwts., and at Valentia, amounting to 20,837 cwts., of a total value of £21,168. That landed at other centres were of a value of £5788. When the spring mackerel fishing flourished about 1865 Kinsale was the centre, and large craft flocked thither from the Isle of Man, from Lowestoft, Cornwall, and France. The local fishermen were at first unprepared, and the Baroness Burdett-Coutts made a loan of £10,000 for the Baltimore district to enable the Cape Clear fishermen to get modern boats. This loan was repaid. The autumn mackerel fishery of 1915 was the worst recorded, and yielded about 53,000 cwts., a decrease of 14,000 cwts. on the figure for the previous

season. The amount realised, however, increased from
£26,000 to nearly £33,000. In addition to the above,
there was in the year referred to about 148 tons
of other fish, principally plaice, black soles, and ray
landed at Dingle (Kerry). There are oyster fisheries
in Tralee, Kinsale, and Waterford, and a mussel
fishery at Castlemaine Harbour (Kerry). The sea-

Lax Weir Salmon Fisheries

weed, which on burning yields " kelp," a source of
potash, is collected from the western coast and the
kelp exported. About 934 tons was exported from
County Clare in 1915.

The inland fisheries are widely known for the
catch of salmon and trout. These fisheries are under
the control of Boards of Conservators. The number
of rod licences decreased during the war, but in
1913 no fewer than 3526 were issued for the whole
country, of which a considerable proportion were for

the southern province. Lismore, Waterford, Kenmare, Waterville, Killarney, and Limerick are the better-known districts for salmon fishing. Grants are made by the Department through their Fisheries Branch to the various Boards of Conservators to assist in the improvement and protection of the inland fisheries. There is a very old and important salmon fishery in the neighbourhood of Limerick, the great " Lax weir " on the Shannon reminding us of the ancient Scandinavian interest in Irish fisheries. The illustrations show the Lax weir and one of the " Cribs " which are fixed in a vertical position in the gaps of the weir. The fish having passed through the narrow vertical opening in the crib cannot return.

Salmon Crib, Lax Weir

DISTINGUISHED MUNSTERMEN

MUNSTER is particularly rich in men of mark. Cork, it has been claimed, stands first among Irish counties in intellectual and artistic achievement. The difficulty of making a selection of representative men for Munster has been accordingly considerable. To her, more than any other province belongs pre-eminence for the number and quality of her native Gaelic bards. Space permits only the inclusion of a few great names; but Aonghus Fionn O'Daly, Geoffrey Fionn O'Daly, Egan O'Rahilly, David O'Bruadair, Tadhg MacBrody, Pierce Fitzgerald, Pierce Ferriter, John O'Tuomy, not to mention many others, are ho sehold names among the Gael. Nor are great scholars and divines wanting. One has only to mention Peter Lombard (d. 1625), Stephen White (d. 1647), Geoffrey of Waterford (d. about 1300), Thomas Hibernicus (fl. 1306), Thomas Carve (d. 1672). In the volume for *Ireland* will be found notices of Robert Boyle, Daniel O'Connell, William Wallace, and Daniel Maclise.

ALLMAN, George James, F.R.S. (1812-98), zoologist and botanist, was born at Cork. He was Professor of Botany in Dublin University from 1844-54, and in Edinburgh from 1855-70, where he was also keeper of the Natural History Museum. He was President of the British Association in 1879. He is noted for his brilliant investigations into the Cœlenterata and Polyzoa. His most important works are *A Monograph of the Freshwater Polyzoa* (1856) and *A Monograph of the Gymnoblastic Hydroids* (1871-72).

m L

BARRY, James, R.A. (1741-1806), the painter, was born at Cork, and studied under West in Dublin. When a young man he attracted the notice of Edmund Burke, who became his friend, and enabled him to complete his studies in France and Italy. His great

John Philpot Curran

achievement was the series of colossal historical paintings illustrating the progress of *Human Culture*, with which he decorated the walls of the Society of Arts in London. His independent nature involved him in constant disputes, and led to his expulsion in 1799 from the Professorship of Painting in the Royal Academy.

BRENDAN, Saint (484-577), called the Voyager, to distinguish him from Brendan of Birr, his fellow-student at Clonard, and, like him, one of the twelve apostles of Ireland, was born at Tralee. The *Navigatio*, with which his name is associated, was one of the most popular legends of the Middle Ages, and was no doubt based on an actual voyage to some of the islands in the Atlantic. He founded the monastery of Clonfert about 553, and visited Columba at Iona in 563.

CURRAN, John Philpot (1750-1817), orator and states-man, was born at Newmarket, Co. Cork. He sat in the Irish Parliament from 1783-97, and was a strong advocate of Reform and Catholic emancipation. It was at the bar, however, that he gained his great repu-tation as an orator and wit. He defended Archibald Hamilton Rowan in 1793, Wolfe Tone in 1798, and others of the United Irishmen. He was Master of the Rolls from 1806-14. His last years, clouded by domestic unhappiness, were spent in London, where he died. He is buried in Glasnevin.

DAVIS, Thomas Osborne (1814-45), poet and patriot, was born at Mallow, Co. Cork, his father, an army surgeon, being of Welsh origin. He was educated at Trinity College, and for a time practised at the bar. An ardent member of the Reform Association, he helped to start *The Nation* newspaper (1842), in which most of his writings appeared. When the New Ireland movement was founded, Davis became its natural leader. He was the loftiest and most inspiring of the national writers. His finest poems are the *Lament for Owen Roe O'Neill*, *Fontenoy*, and *The Sack of Baltimore*.

DOWDEN, Edward (1843-1913), Shakespearean scholar

and critic, was born at Cork. When only twenty-four he became Professor of English Literature in Dublin University, which post he held until his death. He published many volumes of critical essays and biographies, but his fame rests on his *Shakespere . . . his Mind and Art* (1875) and his *Life of Shelley* (1886).

GOUGH, Sir Hugh (1779-1869), First Viscount and Field-Marshal, was born at Limerick. He is said to have commanded in more general actions than any British general with the exception of Wellington. He served through the Peninsular War, and the China War (1842), for his services in which he was created a baronet. As commander-in-chief in India he defeated the Mahrattas (1843). After his successful conduct of the Sikh War (1845-49) he was raised to the peerage and granted an annual pension of £4000.

GRIFFIN, Gerald (1803-40), novelist and poet, was born at Limerick. He is best known by his novel *The Collegians*, which was dramatised by Dion Boucicault as *The Colleen Bawn* in 1828, and his *Tales of the Munster Festivals*. He wrote many ballads and lyrics of great delicacy and beauty: *Eileen Aroon*, *Gile Machree*, and *Lines to a Seagull* are favourites. He became a Christian Brother in 1838.

HARVEY, William Henry (1811-66), botanist, was born at Summerville, Co. Limerick. His discovery, when a youth, of a new moss led to a life-long acquaintance with Sir William Hooker. In 1835 he left Ireland for Capetown, where he succeeded his brother as Colonial Treasurer, returning home in 1842 owing to ill-health, which dogged him throughout life. In 1844 he became Curator of the Dublin University Herbarium, and in 1856 Professor of Botany. He was the greatest Irish

Field-Marshal Viscount Gough

botanist, and the leading authority on Algæ. He published the *Flora* of several continents. His best-known works are *Manual of British Algæ* (1841) and *Phycologia Britannica : a History of British Seaweeds* (1846-51).

HINCKS, Edward, D.D. (1792-1866), the Egyptologist, was born at Cork. He was a Fellow of Trinity College, but, passed over by the university, retired to a living in Killyleagh, Co. Down. In this obscure parish he laboured for forty years, and won European fame by his investigations into the language of the Egyptian hieroglyphics and the cuneiform inscriptions. Among many brilliant discoveries, the determination of the numerals and the names Sennacherib and Nebuchadnezzar are due to him. His work appeared in the *Transactions of the Royal Irish Academy.* He was awarded the Prussian order Pour le mérite.

HOGAN, John (1800-58), the eminent sculptor, was born at Tallow, Co. Waterford. In 1824 he was sent by friends to Rome to perfect his studies, and there he married and settled down for twenty-four years, when the revolution drove him back to Ireland. The last ten years of his life were spent in Dublin. Among his chief works are the *Drunken Faun*, which won the admiration of the great Thorwaldsen, the *Dead Christ* in the Carmelite Church, Clarendon Street, and the statues of *Drummond, O'Connell, Davis*, and *Bishop Doyle*.

KEATING, Geoffrey, D.D. (1570-1650), historian, born at Burgess in Tipperary, of Norman descent, and educated at Bordeaux, is perhaps the best-known name in modern native Irish literature. His *History of Ireland* (Forus Feasa ar Éirinn), compiled from the oldest manuscript sources, is his chief work. An English paraphrase of it by O'Conor (1723) was until recent times the principal authority for most writers on early Irish history. The Irish text, widely circulated in MS. copies down to the Famine, has since been carefully edited and translated. Another well-known work by Keating, which now ranks as a classic, is his *Three Shafts of Death* (Trí Biorghaoithe an Bháis). He is one of the greatest masters of Irish prose, and at the same time a poet of distinction.

KICKHAM, Charles Joseph (1828-82), poet and novelist, was born at Mullinahone in Tipperary. One of the leaders of the Fenian movement, he was sentenced to fourteen years' imprisonment in 1865. His fame rests on his powerful novel *Knocknagow*.

MERRYMAN, Bryan (1747-1805), poet, was born at Clondagach near Ennis, and was by profession a schoolmaster. His chief work, *Cúirt an Meadhon Oidhche* (The Midnight Court), a satirical poem of great power, is generally regarded as the most original product of modern Gaelic literature. It has been elaborately edited and translated into German by the late Ludwig Stern, Director of the Imperial Library, Berlin.

MULREADY, William, R.A. (1786-1863), genre painter, was born at Ennis, Co. Clare. When a boy, his father, who was a leather breeches maker, removed to London. The great sculptor Banks, discerning the boy's talent gave him drawing lessons in his studio, and afterwards he entered the schools of the Royal Academy. He rapidly attained a foremost place in his profession. His *Idle Boys* procured his election as A.R.A. in 1915, and within a year he was made a full member, a rare distinction. His work is distinguished by the perfect drawing, minute and exquisite finish, and brilliant colouring. Usually only one of his small pictures was exhibited annually. Most of them have become the property of the nation, and are now in South Kensington. The most celebrated is *Choosing the Wedding Gown* (1846).

O'CURRY, Eugene (1794-1862), Irish scholar, was born at Dunaha, near Carrigaholt, Co. Clare, his father, a small farmer, being an enthusiastic Gael. In 1834 a life of uncongenial labour was terminated for O'Curry by a post in the Ordnance Survey under Petrie [*q.v. Leinster* volume], where his duties, involving research in the Dublin libraries, enabled him to lay the foundation of his unrivalled knowledge of ancient Irish manuscripts. On the establishment of the Catholic University in 1854, he was appointed to the chair of Irish History and Archæology. His lectures, published as *Manuscript Materials for Ancient Irish History* (1861) and *On the Manners and Customs of the Ancient Irish* (1873), marked an era in the study of Irish civilisation, and are still indispensable. In conjunction with O'Donovan [*q.v. Ireland* volume] he transcribed and translated the *Ancient Laws of Ireland*, death overtaking both these illustrious scholars as they were preparing the first volumes for the press.

O'DALY, Donough Mór (d. 1244), in Irish Donnchadh mór Ó Dálaigh, one of the greatest of native Munster poets, " who never was and never will be surpassed," according to the Four Masters, was a native of Clare, and lived at Finnyvarra. His poems are mostly religious, many being in praise of the Virgin. He is buried in the monastery of Boyle.

O'FIHELLY, Maurice (d. 1513), Archbishop of Tuam

generally known as Maurice *de Portu* or *de Hibernia*,
was a native of Cork.   He studied at Oxford, and, enter-
ing the Franciscan Order, became Regent of the Schools
at Mil n and Padua.   He was a noted classical scholar,

Rev. George Salmon, D.D.

aiding in the production of the classics in one of the
great printing houses at Venice.   He published many
of the works of *Duns Scotus*, with commentaries, at
Venice and Paris, between 1497 and 1513.   He was
appointed Archbishop of Tuam in 1506.

O'SULLIVAN, Owen Roe (*c.* 1748-84), the most popular

native Munster poet, was born at Meentogues, near Killarney. He served for a time in the British navy, taking part in the Battle of the Saintes in 1782, under Rodney, to whom one of his odes is addressed. A writer

Luke Wadding

of great power and variety, his stirring Jacobite songs are immensely popular in the South of Ireland.

SALMON, George, D.D., F.R.S. (1819-1904), mathematician and divine, was born at Cork. He became a Fellow of Trinity College in 1841, his first mathematical paper appearing in 1844. His chief works, translated into many languages, are *Conic Sections* (1847), which still remains the principal text-book on the subject ; *Higher Plane Curves* (1852), *Modern Higher Algebra* (1859), and *Geometry of Three Dimensions* (1862). From 1866 to 1888, when he became Provost, he was Regius Professor of Divinity in Dublin University. As a theologian he is best known by his *Introduction to the New Testament* (1885).

WADDING, Luke (1588-1657), historian and philosopher, was born at Waterford and educated at Lisbon, becoming a member of the Franciscan Order. His life was spent almost wholly in Rome, where he founded the College of St Isidore in 1625. It was at his instance that Rinuccini was sent as papal nuncio to Ireland in 1642. He was a voluminous writer, his most important works being the history of his own Order, *Annales Minorum Ordinum Franciscanorum* (1625-54) and his edition of the works of *Duns Scotus* in 12 folio volumes, prepared in 1639. The remarkable portrait of him by Ribera (Spagnoletto) here reproduced is in the National Portrait Gallery, Dublin.

INDEX